Company's Coming

Tonight!

MAGICAL MEALS ON SHORT NOTICE

Jean Paré

SPECIAL OCCASION SERIES

Anise Crème Brulée, page 145

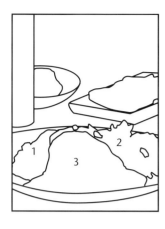

Front Cover
1. Creamy Garlic Mashed
   Potatoes, page 103
2. Citrus Pecan Salad,
   page 110
3. Mushroom Madeira
   Tenderloin, page 11

Company's Coming—Tonight!

First Printing October 2008

Library and Archives Canada Cataloguing in Publication

Paré, Jean, date-
Company's coming tonight : magical meals on short notice / Jean Paré.
(Special occasion series)
Includes index.
ISBN 978-1-897069-49-3
1. Cookery. 2. Menus. 3. Entertaining. I. Title. II. Series.
TX833.5.P373 2008   641.5   C2008-900595-3

Published by
Company's Coming Publishing Limited
2311 – 96 Street
Edmonton, Alberta, Canada T6N 1G3
Tel: 780-450-6223   Fax: 780-450-1857
www.companyscoming.com

Company's Coming is a registered trademark owned by Company's Coming Publishing Limited

Printed in China

We acknowledge the financial support of the Government of Canada through the Book Publishing Industry Development Program (BPIDP) for our publishing activities.

Company's Coming—Tonight! was created thanks to the dedicated efforts of the people and organizations listed below.

COMPANY'S COMING PUBLISHING LIMITED

Author	Jean Paré
President	Grant Lovig
Associate Publisher	Roxanne Higuchi
Creative Director	Heather Markham
Editorial Director	Diane Barton
Research & Development Manager	Jill Corbett
Editors	Janet Fowler Amy Hough
Senior Food Editor	Lynda Elsenheimer
Designer	Natasha Paterson
Photography Director	Jason Symington
Food Editors	Mary Anne Korn Eleana Yun
Recipe Editors	Janet Fowler Aaron Taylor
Contributors	Jessica Assaly Rebecca Kostiuk Laurie Stempfle
Copyeditor	Laurie Penner
Proofreader	Jennifer Sayers Bagjer
Senior Tester	James Bullock
Testers	Allison Dosman Audrey Smetaniuk
Photographer	Stephe Tate Photo
Food Stylist	Ashley Billey
Prop Stylist	Snez Ferenac
Prep Assistant	Linda Dobos
Nutritionist	Vera Mazurak, Ph.D.

We gratefully acknowledge the following suppliers for their generous support of our Test and Photography Kitchens:

Broil King Barbecues
Corelle®
Hamilton Beach® Canada
Lagostina®
Proctor Silex® Canada
Tupperware®

Our special thanks to the following businesses for providing props for photography:

Danesco Inc.	Pier 1 Imports®
Pfaltzgraff Canada	Winners Stores
Mikasa Home Store	Emile Henry
Stokes	Corelle®
Cherison Enterprises Inc.	Totally Bamboo
Out of the Fire Studio	Klass Works

Foreword

When guests come over to my house for dinner, it's always a special occasion. Out come the good china, my antique silver candle holders and a freshly pressed table cloth. I really enjoy every aspect of entertaining—from planning the menu to setting the ambience to watching my friends' and family's reactions to each special course I serve. I believe in making my guests feel pampered and at ease—but I also believe the host should have some fun too!

Company's Coming—Tonight! is designed for people who want to put on a dinner party with flair, but without too much rush and fuss—even if they only have a day's notice to pull everything together. In this colourful collection, we've compiled everything you need for a special night in, such as recipes that are practical to make but have a little extra something to make them truly "guest worthy." We've even included menu suggestions, decorating inspiration and music ideas—everything you need to make your guests feel like you've pulled out all the stops especially for them.

Trust me, with *Company's Coming—Tonight!* it's easy to put on a stellar dinner party. Follow our suggestions to the letter or mix and match recipes for your own creative touch. Tonight's going to be an evening to remember!

Jean Paré

How this book is organized

MARVELLOUS MAINS

We've organized this book based on 30 outstanding main course entrees—or, as we like to call them, your "marvellous mains." They run the gamut from beef, chicken, pork and seafood to meatless. Each main course has a theme based on the type of cuisine, such as Asian or southwestern, the type of gathering, such as a casual movie night or an autumn feast, or a special flavour that dominates, such as maple sweetness or chili pepper spice.

Nutrition Information Guidelines

Each recipe is analyzed using the most current version of the Canadian Nutrient File from Health Canada, which is based on the United States Department of Agriculture (USDA) Nutrient Database.

- If more than one ingredient is listed (such as "butter or hard margarine"), or if a range is given (1 – 2 tsp., 5 – 10 mL), only the first ingredient or first amount is analyzed.
- For meat, poultry and fish, the serving size per person is based on the recommended 4 oz. (113 g) uncooked weight (without bone), which is 2 – 3 oz. (57 – 85 g) cooked weight (without bone)—approximately the size of a deck of playing cards.
- Milk used is 1% M.F. (milk fat), unless otherwise stated.
- Cooking oil used is canola oil, unless otherwise stated.
- Ingredients indicating "sprinkle," "optional," or "for garnish" are not included in the nutrition information.
- The fat in recipes and combination foods can vary greatly depending on the sources and types of fats used in each specific ingredient. For these reasons, the amount of saturated, monounsaturated and polyunsaturated fats may not add up to the total fat content.

Vera C. Mazurak, Ph.D., Nutritionist

NUMBER OF GUESTS

Each entree is made to serve either four, six, eight, ten or twelve people. So, when planning your menu, simply go to the index, check which entrees are made for the number of friends you're expecting and make your choice. This is not to say you're limited to only those recipes—each main course was designed so it could be easily halved or doubled if need be.

PERFECT PAIRINGS

What good is a marvellous main without the perfect pairings to help make it shine? For each main course we have made menu suggestions for beverages, appetizers, sides and desserts you can make to complete a perfectly complementary meal. But don't feel you have to follow our suggestions. We've included loads of extra recipes that aren't a part of any particular menu—so you're bound to find something extraordinary to go with your entree.

"SIMPLIFY" TIPS

Because we want you to enjoy creating this wonderful meal for your nearest and dearest, we've added lots of tips that will make dinner that much easier if you're feeling a little pressed for time. They can be as easy as substituting a bakery-made dessert for the one we've suggested, or they might be hints on how to do some prep ahead of time.

Table of Contents

Roasted Garlic Focaccia, page 97

Pear Masala Crepes, page 157

Crab and Artichoke Pâtè, page 73

Pepper Chicken Kabobs, page 23

Marvellous Mains

Grilled Salmon With Mango Chutney, page 35

HEAVENLY HAVANA

The nuances of Mexican food are strong in our minds, but what about the food of its island neighbour, Cuba? With delicious roast meats, verde sauces and a focus on the piquant freshness of lime, Cuba's cuisine is certainly worthy of your guests' attention. The tangy highlight of the evening is a tender flank steak wonderfully flavoured with a lime marinade. For added interest, it's served with a chipotle and sweet onion salsa loaded with fresh cilantro.

SIMPLIFY: Instead of preparing the Chipotle Salsa, substitute with your favourite premade brand.

For a quick and easy dessert, pour coffee-flavoured liqueur over a scoop of chocolate ice cream.

PRESENTATION IDEA: Serve the sliced steak on a platter with the salsa spooned delicately over the slices.

For a further exploration
of our take on Cuban
fare, we suggest:

APPETIZER

Citrus Shrimp Salad
    Ceviche, page 76

SIDE DISH

Spicy Confetti Salad,
    page 137

BEVERAGE

Mojitos,
    page 93

Lime Chipotle Flank Steak With Chipotle Salsa

Lime, chipotle pepper and cilantro make this combination of grilled steak and salsa a feast for the taste buds!

CHIPOTLE SALSA

Olive oil	2 tbsp.	30 mL
Chopped sweet onion	1 1/2 cups	375 mL
Garlic cloves, minced	3	3
Fresh cilantro or parsley, lightly packed	1/3 cup	75 mL
Chopped chipotle peppers in adobo sauce (see Tip, page 125)	1 tsp.	5 mL
Large Roma (plum) tomatoes, quartered, seeds removed	6	6
Red wine vinegar	2 tbsp.	30 mL
Granulated sugar	1 tsp.	5 mL
Salt	1 tsp.	5 mL

STEAK

Lime juice	1/2 cup	125 mL
Garlic cloves, minced (or 3/4 tsp., 4 mL, powder)	3	3
Grated lime zest (see Tip, page 122)	1 tbsp.	15 mL
Finely chopped chipotle peppers in adobo sauce (see Tip, page 125)	2 tsp.	10 mL
Ground coriander	1 tsp.	5 mL
Ground cumin	1 tsp.	5 mL
Salt	1 tsp.	5 mL
Flank steak	1 1/2 lbs.	680 g

Chipotle Salsa: Heat olive oil in medium frying pan on medium. Add onion. Cook for 15 to 20 minutes, stirring often, until caramelized. Add garlic. Heat and stir for 1 to 2 minutes until fragrant.

Put cilantro and chipotle pepper into food processor. Process with on/off motion until coarsely chopped. Add tomato and onion mixture. Process with on/off motion until coarsely chopped. Transfer to medium bowl.

Add next 3 ingredients. Stir. Let stand for 30 minutes to blend flavours. Makes about 2 cups (500 mL) salsa.

Steak: Combine first 7 ingredients in small bowl.

Put steak into large resealable freezer bag. Add lime mixture. Seal bag. Turn until coated. Let stand in refrigerator for 2 to 3 hours, turning occasionally. Drain lime mixture into small saucepan. Bring to a boil. Reduce heat to medium-low. Simmer, uncovered, for 5 minutes. Preheat gas barbecue to high. Cook steak on greased grill for 5 to 7 minutes per side, brushing with reserved lime mixture, for medium-rare or until desired doneness. Transfer to cutting board. Cover with foil. Let stand for 10 minutes. Cut steak diagonally, across the grain, on a sharp angle into very thin slices. Serve with Chipotle Salsa. Serves 6.

1 serving: 280 Calories; 14.8 g Total Fat (7.5 g Mono, 0.9 g Poly, 4.9 g Sat); 48 g Cholesterol; 11 g Carbohydrate; 2 g Fibre; 26 g Protein; 869 mg Sodium

Pictured at left.

WINTER WONDERFUL

Our appetites seem to change during the winter. We opt for more wholesome, heartier fare in an attempt to counterbalance the cold outside. Yet we also yearn for flavour and freshness wherever we can get it. Winter can be quite wonderful when we allow ourselves to indulge in the pure comfort that food can give us. Our ode to winter eating features an entree of beef tenderloin with a luscious Madeira and mushroom sauce.

SIMPLIFY: Instead of presenting the crepes for dessert, make the Orange Butter Sauce and serve over store-bought cheesecake.

DRINK SUGGESTION: Serve your meal with a full-bodied wine such as a Shiraz or Cabernet Sauvignon.

PRESENTATION IDEA: If you're having a long evening in, the perfect after-dinner complement to this meal would be a cheese plate served with nuts, figs and dates, accompanied by a glass of Madeira or port.

Mushroom Madeira Tenderloin

Premium beef roast with a luxurious Madeira sauce will definitely be the star attraction of the evening!

Beef tenderloin roast	3 – 3 1/2 lbs.	1.4 – 1.6 kg
Salt, sprinkle		
Pepper, sprinkle		
MUSHROOM MADEIRA SAUCE		
Butter (or hard margarine)	1/4 cup	60 mL
Finely chopped onion	1/2 cup	125 mL
Garlic clove, minced	1	1
(or 1/4 tsp., 1 mL, powder)		
Sliced fresh brown mushrooms	4 cups	1 L
All-purpose flour	1/4 cup	60 mL
Prepared beef broth	1 1/4 cups	300 mL
Madeira wine	1/2 cup	125 mL
Salt	1/4 tsp.	1 mL
Pepper	1/4 tsp.	1 mL

Place roast on greased wire rack set in 9 x 13 inch (22 x 33 cm) baking dish. Sprinkle with salt and pepper. Bake, uncovered, in 475°F (240°C) oven for about 15 minutes until browned. Reduce heat to 325°F (160°C). Cook for about 75 minutes until meat thermometer inserted into thickest part of roast reads 140°F (60°C) for medium-rare or until desired doneness. Transfer to cutting board. Cover with foil. Let stand for 10 minutes.

Mushroom Madeira Sauce: Melt butter in large frying pan on medium. Add onion and garlic. Cook for about 5 minutes, stirring often, until onion is softened.

Add mushrooms. Cook for about 10 minutes, stirring occasionally, until mushrooms are browned and liquid is evaporated.

Add flour. Heat and stir for 1 minute.

Slowly add broth and wine, stirring constantly, until smooth. Heat and stir until boiling and thickened. Add salt and pepper. Stir. Makes about 2 2/3 cups (650 mL) sauce. Slice roast. Serve with Mushroom Madeira Sauce. Serves 10.

1 serving: 239 Calories; 12.4 g Total Fat (4.2 g Mono, 0.5 g Poly, 5.8 g Sat); 63 mg Cholesterol; 6 g Carbohydrate; 1 g Fibre; 22 g Protein; 284 mg Sodium

Pictured on front cover and at left.

To complete a menu free of the winter blues, we suggest:

APPETIZER

Baked Chèvre Crostini, page 77

SIDE DISHES

Citrus Pecan Salad, page 110

Creamy Garlic Mashed Potatoes, page 103

DESSERT

Simple Crepes Suzette, page 163

BEVERAGE

Kir Royale, page 93

Creamy Garlic Mashed Potatoes

Simple Crepes Suzette

Kir Royale

PLAY IT AGAIN, SAM

A dinner fit for Humphrey Bogart and Ingrid Bergman in *Casablanca!* Tonight is all about glamour and the heady intrigue of far-off places such as the African coast. The star performance of your evening will come from a Moroccan Pot Roast, laden with rich, exhilarating flavours.

SIMPLIFY: If you're short on time, use frozen mixed vegetables or buy a couscous salad from your favourite deli.

For dessert, replace Cinnamon Ginger Oranges with cut-up fresh oranges and serve with the baklava.

DRINK SUGGESTION: Serve a quality ice wine with dessert, or how about a Moroccan mint tea blend?

Moroccan Pot Roast

Taste Morocco in this classic dish—fruity sweetness paired with the warm spices of cinnamon, cumin and ginger. You'll have plenty of gravy to serve with this tender beef.

Salt	1/4 tsp.	1 mL
Pepper	1/4 tsp.	1 mL
Boneless beef cross-rib roast	3 lbs.	1.4 kg
Cooking oil	1 tbsp.	15 mL
Cooking oil	1 tsp.	5 mL
Chopped onion	1 cup	250 mL
Garlic cloves, minced	2	2
(or 1/2 tsp., 2 mL, powder)		
Brown sugar, packed	1 tsp.	5 mL
Ground cinnamon	1 tsp.	5 mL
Ground cumin	1 tsp.	5 mL
Ground ginger	1 tsp.	5 mL
Salt	1/2 tsp.	2 mL
Pepper	1/2 tsp.	2 mL
Prepared beef broth	2 cups	500 mL
Chopped dried apricot	1/2 cup	125 mL
Raisins	1/2 cup	125 mL
All-purpose flour	2 tbsp.	30 mL

Sprinkle salt and pepper over roast. Heat first amount of cooking oil in Dutch oven on medium-high. Add roast. Cook, uncovered, for 1 to 2 minutes per side until browned. Transfer to plate. Reduce heat to medium.

Heat second amount of cooking oil in same Dutch oven. Add onion. Cook, uncovered, for 5 to 10 minutes, stirring often, until softened.

Add next 7 ingredients. Heat and stir for about 1 minute until fragrant.

Add next 3 ingredients. Bring to a boil, stirring constantly and scraping any brown bits from bottom of pot. Add roast. Bake, covered, in 300°F (150°C) oven for 1 1/2 to 2 hours until tender. Transfer roast to cutting board. Cover with foil. Let stand for 10 minutes. Slice roast.

Strain cooking liquid through sieve set over medium saucepan. Reserve solids. Skim and discard any fat from surface of liquid (see Tip). Stir 1/4 cup (60 mL) liquid into flour in small cup until smooth. Bring remaining liquid to a boil. Slowly add flour mixture, stirring constantly with whisk. Heat and stir until boiling and thickened. Add reserved solids. Stir. Serve with roast. Serves 6.

1 serving: 703 Calories; 48.9 g Total Fat (22.3 g Mono, 2.7 g Poly, 19.0 g Sat); 146 mg Cholesterol; 25 g Carbohydrate; 40 g Fibre; 30 g Protein; 775 mg Sodium

Pictured at left.

Glam it up, Casablanca-style with the following:

SIDE DISHES

Vegetable Bulgur, page 130

Carrot And Beet Salad, page 142

DESSERTS

Cinnamon Ginger Oranges, page 147

Baklava Rosettes, page 153

Vegetable Bulgur

Cinnamon Ginger Oranges

CHIT CHAT AND ALL THAT

It's all about flavour and colour. This casual, down-home meal is ideal for a relaxing weekend get-together. Gather your friends to watch the game or just for a long, overdue chat. When you serve it buffet-style, there's no fuss and no muss.

SIMPLIFY: Try serving crusty rolls or mashed potatoes in place of the dumplings.

If you're making Braised Carrots And Leeks, omit the leeks.

DRINK SUGGESTION: Lager, ale or dark beer make for a satisfying accompaniment.

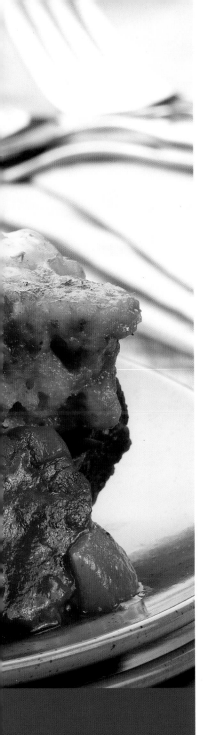

Braised Beef With Parsley Dumplings

A bistro-style supper that uses everyday ingredients. It's destined to become a family favourite.

Cooking oil	2 tsp.	10 mL
Boneless beef cross-rib roast (or beef cross-rib steak), cut into 1 1/2 inch (3.8 cm) pieces	2 – 3 lbs.	900 g – 1.4 kg
Cooking oil	2 tsp.	10 mL
Coarsely chopped onion	3 cups	750 mL
Ketchup	1 1/4 cups	300 mL
Dry (or alcohol-free) red wine	2/3 cup	150 mL
Prepared beef broth	1/2 cup	125 mL
Balsamic vinegar	1 tsp.	5 mL
Salt	1/2 tsp.	2 mL
Pepper	1/2 tsp.	2 mL
Bay leaves	3	3
PARSLEY DUMPLINGS		
All-purpose flour	2 cups	500 mL
Chopped fresh parsley (or 1 tbsp., 15 mL, flakes)	1/4 cup	60 mL
Baking powder	4 tsp.	20 mL
Seasoned salt	1 1/2 tsp.	7 mL
Garlic powder	1/4 tsp.	1 mL
Large egg, fork-beaten	1	1
Milk	1 cup	250 mL
Cooking oil	2 tbsp.	30 mL

Heat cooking oil in large frying pan on medium-high. Add beef. Cook for about 5 minutes, stirring occasionally, until browned. Transfer to plate. Reduce heat to medium.

Add second amount of cooking oil to same frying pan. Add onion. Cook for about 10 minutes, stirring often, until softened and browned. Layer beef and onion in 4 to 5 quart (4 to 5 L) oval slow cooker.

Combine next 6 ingredients in medium bowl. Pour over beef. Add bay leaves. Cook, covered, on Low for 6 to 8 hours or on High for 3 to 4 hours until beef is tender. Discard bay leaves.

Parsley Dumplings: Measure first 5 ingredients into medium bowl. Stir. Make a well in centre.

Combine remaining 3 ingredients in small bowl. Add to well. Stir until just moistened. Drop 12 large spoonfuls of batter over beef mixture. Cook, covered, on High for about 30 minutes until wooden pick inserted in centre of dumpling comes out clean. Makes about 5 cups (1.25 L) beef and 12 dumplings. Serves 6.

1 serving: 729 Calories; 39.5 g Total Fat (18.7 g Mono, 3.7 g Poly, 13.6 g Sat); 131 mg Cholesterol; 55 g Carbohydrate; 3 g Fibre; 34 g Protein; 1501 mg Sodium

Pictured at left.

For the perfect casual evening, we suggest:

APPETIZER
Crab And Artichoke Pâté, page 73

SIDE DISH
Braised Carrots And Leeks, page 141

DESSERT
Rum Raisin Apple Enchiladas, page 164

OOM-PA-PA OOMPH

Set this dish in front of your guests for a festive Oktoberfest atmosphere—any time of year! Although the name sounds as though it would be difficult to make, it's really not. For added ease, you can prepare this rich, robust dish in advance.

SIMPLIFY: Instead of spaetzle, try serving buttered egg noodles with poppy seeds.

Buy a Black Forest cake from your favourite bakery instead of making the Black Forest Cherry Clafouti.

DECORATING IDEA: If you have any European-style dinnerware, this is the time to use it.

Top Left: Dressed-Up Roasted
    Vegetables
Top Right: Spaetzle With
    Caramelized Onions
Bottom: Sauerbraten Rouladen

Sauerbraten Rouladen

We've taken a German specialty of slow-simmered beef in a sweet-and-sour sauce and wrapped it around a savoury bread filling—and yes, the gingersnap crumbs are traditional.

Bacon slices, diced	3	3
Box of stove-top stuffing mix	4 1/4 oz.	120 g
Beef rouladen steaks (about 1 1/2 lbs., 680 g)	6	6
Large dill pickle, cut lengthwise into 6 spears	1	1
Salt	1/2 tsp.	2 mL
Pepper	1/4 tsp.	1 mL
Cooking oil	1 tbsp.	15 mL
Cooking oil	2 tsp.	10 mL
Chopped onion	2 cups	500 mL
Baby carrots	2 cups	500 mL
Prepared beef broth	2 cups	500 mL
Crushed gingersnap cookies	1/4 cup	60 mL
Dry (or alcohol-free) red wine	1/4 cup	60 mL
Red wine vinegar	1/4 cup	60 mL
Brown sugar, packed	2 tbsp.	30 mL
Bay leaves	2	2
Ground allspice	1/2 tsp.	2 mL
Cornstarch	2 tsp.	10 mL
Water	2 tbsp.	30 mL

Cook bacon in large frying pan on medium until crisp. Transfer to paper towel-lined plate to drain. Drain and discard drippings from pan.

Prepare stuffing mix according to package directions, using half the liquid called for. Add bacon. Toss.

Arrange steaks on work surface. Lay 1 pickle spear crosswise across centre of each steak. Spoon about 1/3 cup (75 mL) stuffing mixture onto wide end of each steak. Starting at wide end, roll to enclose stuffing. Secure with wooden picks. Sprinkle with salt and pepper.

Heat first amount of cooking oil in same frying pan on medium-high. Add steak rolls. Cook for about 5 minutes, turning often, until browned on all sides. Transfer to plate. Reduce heat to medium.

Add second amount of cooking oil to same frying pan. Add onion. Cook for about 5 minutes, stirring often, until softened and browned.

Add next 8 ingredients. Stir, scraping any brown bits from bottom of pan. Bring to a boil. Reduce heat to medium-low. Add steak rolls. Cook, covered, turning occasionally, for about 1 hour until beef is tender. Transfer steak rolls to plate. Cover to keep warm. Discard bay leaves. Increase heat to medium.

Stir cornstarch into water in small cup. Add to broth mixture. Heat and stir until boiling and thickened. Add steak rolls. Turn to coat. Serves 6.

1 serving: 434 Calories; 16.7 g Total Fat (6.8 g Mono, 1.8 g Poly, 4.6 g Sat); 49 mg Cholesterol; 38 g Carbohydrate; 3 g Fibre; 30 g Protein; 1419 mg Sodium

Pictured at left.

Stick with the Bavarian theme and serve:

SIDE DISHES

Spaetzle With Caramelized Onions, page 115

Dressed-Up Roasted Vegetables, page 143

DESSERT

Black Forest Cherry Clafouti, page 160

BEVERAGE

Rich Viennese Coffee, page 95

HEARTH AND HOME

When autumn leaves begin to fall and the landscape is coloured in shades of crimson, yellow and orange, one can't fight the urge to nestle inside by the fire and enjoy some nourishing home cooking. For those crisp fall nights, we've chosen a smoky turkey stew packed with potatoes, carrots and celery.

SIMPLIFY: Instead of making the focaccia, just buy some from your local bakery and warm in the oven before serving.

Instead of making the dessert, serve gourmet ice cream topped with crushed pretzels and nuts.

MUSIC SUGGESTION: Bring out the old-time country favourites like Patsy Cline, Hank Williams Sr., Jimmie Rodgers and Lefty Frizzell.

Rustic Turkey Stew

This rustic stew of tender turkey and vegetables has plenty of rich-tasting, smoky gravy and will leave your guests heartily fed.

Bacon slices, diced	3	3
All-purpose flour	1/2 cup	125 mL
Salt	1/2 tsp.	2 mL
Pepper	1/2 tsp.	2 mL
Boneless, skinless turkey thighs, cut into 2 inch (5 cm) pieces	1 lb.	454 g
Cooking oil	1 tbsp.	15 mL
Cooking oil	2 tsp.	10 mL
Sliced fresh white mushrooms	2 cups	500 mL
Chopped onion	1 cup	250 mL
Garlic clove, minced (or 1/4 tsp., 1 mL, powder)	1	1
Dry (or alcohol-free) white wine	1/2 cup	125 mL
Prepared chicken broth	2 1/2 cups	625 mL
Baby potatoes, larger ones cut in half	1 lb.	454 g
Sliced carrot	1 cup	250 mL
Sliced celery	1 cup	250 mL
Bay leaf	1	1

Cook bacon in large frying pan on medium until crisp. Transfer with slotted spoon to paper towel-lined plate to drain. Discard drippings. Transfer bacon to 3 1/2 to 4 quart (3.5 to 4 L) slow cooker.

Combine next 3 ingredients in large resealable freezer bag. Add half of turkey. Seal bag. Toss until coated. Remove turkey to plate. Repeat with remaining turkey. Reserve any remaining flour mixture.

Heat first amount of cooking oil in same frying pan on medium-high. Add turkey. Cook for about 5 minutes, stirring occasionally, until browned. Transfer to slow cooker using slotted spoon. Reduce heat to medium.

Add next 4 ingredients to same frying pan. Cook for 5 to 10 minutes, stirring often, until onion is softened. Sprinkle with reserved flour mixture. Heat and stir for 1 minute.

Slowly add wine, stirring constantly and scraping any brown bits from bottom of pan. Add broth. Stir. Add to slow cooker.

Add next 3 ingredients. Stir. Add bay leaf. Cook, covered, on Low for 6 to 7 hours or on High for 3 to 3 1/2 hours. Discard bay leaf. Makes about 8 cups (2 L). Serves 4.

1 serving: 421 Calories; 12.3 g Total Fat (4.5 g Mono, 2.2 g Poly, 1.3 g Sat); 5 mg Cholesterol; 43 g Carbohydrate; 4 g Fibre; 28 g Protein; 1387 mg Sodium

Pictured at left.

To complete a menu of hearty, homey goodness, we suggest:

SIDE DISHES
Tomato Basil Salad, page 123

Roasted Garlic Focaccia, page 97

DESSERT
Butter Crunch Ice Cream Squares, page 155

Roasted Garlic Focaccia

Butter Crunch Ice Cream Squares

MEDITERRANEAN MUSINGS

When you daydream about other climes, do you picture yourself on the Mediterranean, drenched in warm sun, staring out onto the glittering ocean, noshing away on all the little delicacies that are so characteristic of the region? Although we can't take you there in body, we can take you there in spirit. Our feature dish is a juicy baked chicken covered in a rustic tomato sauce with olives and fresh oregano.

SIMPLIFY: Replace the Feta Artichoke Mini Pockets with mini pita pockets filled with ready-made artichoke dip, thickened with feta.

Instead of making the Eggplant Zucchini Bake, toss steamed green beans with diced tomatoes and chopped fresh oregano.

DECORATING IDEA: Give your table a rustic feeling with a red and white table cloth. Beside every setting, place a tiny bunch of fragrant dried herbs tied with a ribbon.

Mediterranean Chicken

Treat your guests to the flavours of the Mediterranean with tender, juicy chicken covered in a rustic sauce of tomatoes, olives and oregano.

Chopped fresh oregano (or 1 tbsp., 15 mL, dried)	1/4 cup	60 mL
Dry (or alcohol-free) white wine	1/4 cup	60 mL
Olive oil	1/4 cup	60 mL
Lemon juice	2 tbsp.	30 mL
Garlic cloves, minced (or 1/2 tsp., 2 mL, powder)	2	2
Grated lemon zest (see Tip, page 122)	2 tsp.	10 mL
Liquid honey	2 tsp.	10 mL
Salt	1/4 tsp.	1 mL
Pepper	1/4 tsp.	1 mL
Boneless, skinless chicken breast halves (4 – 6 oz., 113 – 170 g, each)	6	6
All-purpose flour	1/4 cup	60 mL
Olive oil	1 tbsp.	15 mL
Olive oil	1 tsp.	5 mL
Chopped onion	1 1/2 cups	375 mL
Can of diced tomatoes (with juice)	14 oz.	398 mL
Medium pitted black olives	3/4 cup	175 mL
Half-and-half cream	3 tbsp.	50 mL
Lemon slices	12	12
Chopped fresh oregano (or 1/2 tsp., 2 mL, dried)	2 tsp.	10 mL

Combine first 9 ingredients in small bowl.

Put chicken into large resealable freezer bag. Add oregano mixture. Seal bag. Turn until coated. Let stand in refrigerator for 1 to 2 hours, turning occasionally. Remove chicken. Set aside remaining oregano mixture. Pat chicken dry with paper towels.

Measure flour onto plate. Press both sides of chicken into flour. Heat second amount of olive oil in large frying pan on medium-high. Add chicken. Cook for 2 to 4 minutes per side until browned. Arrange chicken in single layer in ungreased 2 quart (2 L) casserole. Set aside. Reduce heat to medium.

Add third amount of olive oil to same frying pan. Add onion. Cook for 5 to 10 minutes, stirring occasionally, until onion is softened.

Add tomatoes and reserved oregano mixture. Bring to a boil. Reduce heat to medium-low. Simmer, uncovered, for about 5 minutes until liquid is reduced.

Add olives and cream. Stir. Pour over chicken. Bake, covered, in 350°F (175°C) oven for about 30 minutes until bubbling and chicken is tender.

Arrange 2 lemon slices over each chicken breast. Sprinkle with oregano. Serves 6.

1 serving: 531 Calories; 22.5 g Total Fat (10.2 g Mono, 2.0 g Poly, 3.3 g Sat); 158 mg Cholesterol; 16 g Carbohydrate; 1 g Fibre; 63 g Protein; 657 mg Sodium

Pictured at left.

To make your daydream complete, we suggest:

APPETIZER
Feta Artichoke Mini Pockets, page 81

SIDE DISHES
Pistachio Pilaf, page 133

Eggplant Zucchini Bake, page 103

BEVERAGE
Fruity Sangria, page 89

MARIACHI MELODIES

Capture the anticipation of an upcoming holiday or reminisce of one that is past by sharing the tastes and colours of Mexico. Envision a slow pace, sharing memories with old friends and settling in for a warm evening of laughs. The perfect main course is smoky, citrus-spiced chicken and veggie skewers—easy to hold or magnificently appealing when set on a bed of rice.

SIMPLIFY: Go easy on yourself by serving tortilla chips with a store-bought shrimp ring, bottled salsa and cheese dip for an appetizer.

Consider replacing the Fiesta Rice with fajita-sized tortillas, warmed in a foil pack on the barbecue.

DRINK SUGGESTION: Try a Mexican beer, such as Corona, with a lime wedge pushed into the top of the bottle.

Pepper Chicken Kabobs

Add some sizzle to your next summer party with these smoky, citrus-spiced chicken and veggie skewers.

Boneless, skinless chicken breast halves, cut into 24 equal pieces	1 lb.	454 g
Medium onion, cut into 24 equal pieces	1	1
Large yellow pepper, cut into 24 equal pieces	1	1
Large red pepper, cut into 24 equal pieces	1	1
Bamboo skewers (8 inches, 20 cm, each), soaked in water for 10 minutes	8	8
Orange juice	1/2 cup	125 mL
Ranch dressing	1/4 cup	60 mL
Garlic cloves, minced (or 1/2 tsp., 2 mL, powder)	2	2
Grated lime zest	2 tsp.	10 mL
Ground cumin	1 tsp.	5 mL
Pepper	1 tsp.	5 mL

Thread first 4 ingredients alternately onto skewers. Place in large shallow dish.

Combine remaining 6 ingredients in small bowl. Pour about 2/3 cup (150 mL) over chicken skewers. Chill remaining orange juice mixture. Turn skewers to coat. Let stand, covered, in refrigerator for 2 hours, turning occasionally. Preheat gas barbecue to medium-high. Remove skewers from orange juice mixture. Discard any orange juice mixture remaining in dish. Cook skewers on greased grill for about 6 minutes per side, brushing with reserved orange juice mixture, until chicken is no longer pink inside and vegetables are tender. Serves 4.

1 serving: 225 Calories; 7.5 g Total Fat (0.5 g Mono, 0.5 g Poly, 1.4 g Sat); 69 mg Cholesterol; 12 g Carbohydrate; 2 g Fibre; 27 g Protein; 164 mg Sodium

Pictured on page 6 and at left.

Continue the celebration of Mexico with the following suggested dishes:

SIDE DISHES

DESSERT

Orange Jicama Salad Fiesta Rice Lime Mango Sorbet

THE DELICIOUS SPICE OF LIFE

The aromas of certain spices just evoke feelings of warmth and serenity. Cumin, star anise, cinnamon and allspice are just a few examples of how the scent of food can trigger wonderful memories of days past. Begin your aromatic feast with a Roasted Spice Chicken delicately flavoured with oregano, garlic, cumin and orange.

SIMPLIFY: Simplify the process by using a packaged rice mix as a side instead of Apple Walnut Quinoa.

Substitute a quality store-bought soup, topped with croutons, instead of Caramelized Onion Yam Soup.

Buy a chai concentrate to make the lattes.

DRINK SUGGESTION: Try it dry with a Chardonnay or medium-dry with a Sauvignon Blanc.

Roasted Spice Chicken

Tender, moist chicken with a complex variety of bold spices makes a dazzling entree to serve your guests.

GARLIC ORANGE PASTE		
Garlic cloves, minced	4	4
Balsamic vinegar	1 tbsp.	15 mL
Butter (or hard margarine), softened	1 tbsp.	15 mL
Dried oregano	1 tbsp.	15 mL
Frozen concentrated orange juice, thawed	1 tbsp.	15 mL
Ground cumin	1 tbsp.	15 mL
Salt	1 tsp.	5 mL
Pepper	1 tsp.	5 mL
Whole chicken	3 lbs.	1.4 kg
Butter (or hard margarine), softened	1 tsp.	5 mL

Garlic Orange Paste: Stir first 8 ingredients in small bowl until mixture forms a smooth paste. Makes about 1/3 cup (75 mL) paste.

Carefully loosen chicken skin on breast and thighs but do not remove. Stuff paste between meat and skin, spreading mixture as evenly as possible. Tie wings with butcher's string close to body. Tie legs to tail. Transfer to greased wire rack set in small roasting pan.

Rub butter over surface of chicken. Bake, covered, in 350°F (175°C) oven for 1 1/4 to 1 1/2 hours until meat thermometer inserted into thickest part of breast reads 180°F (83°C). Remove chicken from oven. Transfer to cutting board. Remove and discard butcher's string. Cover with foil. Let stand for 10 minutes before carving. Serves 4.

1 serving: 446 Calories; 26.2 g Total Fat (9.6 g Mono, 5.0 g Poly, 8.5 g Sat); 152 mg Cholesterol; 5 g Carbohydrate; 1 g Fibre; 45 g Protein; 750 mg Sodium

Pictured at left.

To keep your meal at its most "scentual," we suggest:

SIDE DISHES

Apple Walnut Quinoa, page 139

Caramelized Onion Sweet Potato Soup, page 127

Steamed broccoli

DESSERT

Anise Crème Brulée, page 145

BEVERAGE

Mint Chai Latte, page 95

Apple Walnut Quinoa   Caramelized Onion Sweet Potato Soup   Anise Crème Brulée

EAT WITH THE BEAT

Sway to the beat of a reggae riff as you get into the mood for a Caribbean-inspired meal. Follow the island philosophy and take life easy with this delightfully spicy and subtly delicious chicken and pork stew.

SIMPLIFY: Instead of making Polenta Triangles, cut a tube of prepared polenta into 1 inch (2.5 cm) slices and brush with melted butter before broiling. Or simply serve the stew over rice.

DECORATING IDEA: Keep it casual. Try serving the stew in an unusual container such as a hollowed-out pumpkin—unique and colourful.

West Indies Stew

The variety of spices in this chicken and pork stew results in a wonderful complexity of flavours that will have your guests asking for more.

Apple cider vinegar	1/4 cup	60 mL
Apple juice	1/4 cup	60 mL
Dried oregano	2 tsp.	10 mL
Garlic cloves, minced (or 1/2 tsp., 2 mL, powder)	2	2
Salt	1 tsp.	5 mL
Dried crushed chilies	1/2 tsp.	2 mL
Ground allspice	1/2 tsp.	2 mL
Ground coriander	1/2 tsp.	2 mL
Boneless, skinless chicken thighs, quartered	1 lb.	454 g
Stewing pork, cubed	1 lb.	454 g
Cooking oil	1 tbsp.	15 mL
Coarsely chopped green pepper	1 1/2 cups	375 mL
Coarsely chopped onion	1 cup	250 mL
Finely grated gingerroot	1 tbsp.	15 mL
Brown sugar, packed	1 tbsp.	15 mL
Chili powder	1 1/2 tsp.	7 mL
Curry powder	1 1/2 tsp.	7 mL
Can of diced tomatoes (with juice)	14 oz.	398 mL
Prepared chicken broth	1 cup	250 mL
Smooth peanut butter	1/4 cup	60 mL
Bay leaf	1	1
Cubed butternut squash (1/2 inch, 12 mm, pieces)	2 cups	500 mL

Combine first 8 ingredients in small bowl.

Put chicken and pork into large resealable freezer bag. Add vinegar mixture. Seal bag. Toss until coated. Let stand in refrigerator for 1 hour, turning occasionally. Remove chicken and pork from vinegar mixture. Reserve remaining vinegar mixture.

Heat cooking oil in Dutch oven on medium-high. Add chicken and pork. Cook, uncovered, in 2 batches, for 5 to 10 minutes per batch, turning occasionally, until browned. Transfer to plate. Cover to keep warm.

Add next 3 ingredients to same Dutch oven. Cook, uncovered, for 3 to 5 minutes, stirring often, until vegetables start to soften.

Add next 3 ingredients. Heat and stir for about 1 minute until fragrant.

Add next 4 ingredients and reserved vinegar mixture. Stir, scraping any brown bits from bottom of pan. Add chicken and pork. Stir. Bring to a boil. Reduce heat to medium-low. Simmer, covered, for 1 hour.

Add squash. Stir. Cook, covered, for about 30 minutes until squash is tender. Discard bay leaf. Makes about 7 cups (1.75 L). Serves 6.

1 serving: 449 Calories; 25.2 g Total Fat (11.2 g Mono, 4.9 g Poly, 6.9 g Sat); 95 mg Cholesterol; 25 g Carbohydrate; 4 g Fibre; 33 g Protein; 911 mg Sodium

Pictured at left.

Go West Indies all the way with the following meal suggestions:

SIDE DISHES

Polenta Triangles, page 99

Island Greens Salad, page 117

DESSERT

Vanilla Spice Rice Pudding, page 158

AUTUMN MOON MIXER

If you're looking for something different to make for Thanksgiving, this is the definitive dish. But, since turkey is not just relegated to special occasions anymore, try this out whenever you're expecting company and really want to impress.

SIMPLIFY: Instead of Braised Fennel Medley, steam some vegetables or serve a salad.

If time is scarce, rather than the Peach Cream Slice, whip up a peach coulis and serve over a quality store-bought cheesecake.

DRINK SUGGESTION: Sweeten the deal with a semi-sweet white wine such as a Riesling or Pinot Grigio.

Turkey Rice Roulade With Fig Stuffing

If you want to serve turkey but don't want the bother of roasting a whole one, make this attractive turkey breast roll with a tasty and unique fig and rice stuffing.

Packages of long grain and wild rice mix (6 1/4 oz., 180 g, each), with seasoning packets	2	2
Butter (or hard margarine)	1 tbsp.	15 mL
Finely chopped dried fig	1 cup	250 mL
Cherry jam	2/3 cup	150 mL
Sliced almonds, toasted (see Tip, page 79)	3 tbsp.	50 mL
Dried thyme	1 tsp.	5 mL
Garlic powder	1/2 tsp.	2 mL
Boneless, skinless turkey breast roasts (1.5 – 2 lbs., 680 – 900 g each)	2	2
Prepared chicken broth	3/4 cup	175 mL
Cornstarch	1 tbsp.	15 mL
Balsamic vinegar	2 tsp.	10 mL
Dried cranberries	1 cup	250 mL

Chopped fresh parsley, for garnish

Combine rice, seasoning packets and butter in medium saucepan. Cook according to package directions. Cool completely. Transfer 1 1/2 cups (375 mL) to medium bowl. Chill remaining rice.

Combine next 5 ingredients in small bowl. Add 2/3 cup (150 mL) fig mixture to rice in bowl. Stir well. Set aside remaining fig mixture.

To butterfly roasts, cut horizontally lengthwise almost, but not quite, through to other side. Open flat. Place between 2 sheets of plastic wrap. Pound with mallet or rolling pin to 3/4 inch (2 cm) thickness. Repeat with remaining roast. Place each roast on 12 x 15 inch (30 x 38 cm) sheet of greased foil. Spread about 1/3 cup (75 mL) rice mixture on each, leaving 1 inch (2.5 cm) edge on top. Roll up from bottom, jelly roll-style, to enclose stuffing. Roll turkey in foil to enclose. Seal edges of foil tightly. Place packages, seam-side up, in ungreased 9 x 9 inch (22 x 22 cm) baking dish. Bake in 350°F (175°C) oven for about 75 minutes until internal temperature reaches 160°F (71°C). Transfer to cutting board. Let stand in foil for 10 minutes (see Note). Cut rolls into 10 slices each.

Combine next 3 ingredients and remaining fig mixture in small saucepan on medium. Heat and stir until boiling and thickened.

Transfer remaining rice to medium microwave-safe bowl. Add cranberries. Stir. Microwave, covered, on high (100%) for 2 to 4 minutes, stirring occasionally, until heated through. Spread on large serving platter.

Sprinkle with parsley. Arrange turkey slices over rice. Drizzle fig mixture over turkey. Serves 10.

1 serving: 533 Calories; 8.9 g Total Fat (1.2 g Mono, 0.4 g Poly, 2.1 g Sat); 135 mg Cholesterol; 58 g Carbohydrate; 2 g Fibre; 57 g Protein; 2096 mg Sodium

Note: The internal temperature should continue to rise upon standing to approximately 170°F (77°C). It is important to allow the temperature to rise before slicing to ensure that the moisture in the meat is properly distributed. Removing the roasts from the oven at 160°F (71°C) avoids overcooking.

Pictured at left.

Liven up your autumn feast with the following menu suggestions:

SIDE DISH
Braised Fennel Medley, page 109

DESSERT
Peaches And Cream Slice, page 152

BEVERAGE
Pink Pineapple Refresher, page 91

CASUAL AND CREATIVE

If a casual dinner is what you're thinking about before an evening out with friends, our Layered Chicken Artichoke Pie will fit the bill. Serve it up buffet-style with the soup and salad or as a main afterwards. In any case, you can't go wrong with the ease of this unique chicken recipe.

SIMPLIFY: Buy a quality pre-made squash soup instead of making Lemon Split Pea Soup.

Whip up a cake from a mix instead of the Pumpkin Pecan Pound Cake.

DRINK SUGGESTION: The dryness of a Chablis is ideal with the chicken.

Left: Layered Chicken
Artichoke Pie
Right: Spinach and
Strawberry Salad

Layered Chicken Artichoke Pie

*Golden layers of phyllo pastry hold a delicious chicken and rice filling.
A show-stopper!*

FILLING

Cooking oil	2 tsp.	10 mL
Lean ground chicken	1 1/2 lbs.	680 g
Cooking oil	1 tsp.	5 mL
Chopped fresh white mushrooms	3 cups	750 mL
Chopped onion	1 cup	250 mL
Paprika	1 tbsp.	15 mL
Dry mustard	1 tsp.	5 mL
Garlic clove, minced (or 1/4 tsp., 1 mL, powder)	1	1
Granulated sugar	1 tsp.	5 mL
Pepper	1/4 tsp.	1 mL
All-purpose flour	2 tbsp.	30 mL
Prepared chicken broth	1 cup	250 mL
Can of artichoke hearts, drained and quartered	14 oz.	398 mL
Can of diced tomatoes (with juice)	14 oz.	398 mL
Sour cream	1/2 cup	125 mL

PIE

Phyllo pastry sheets, thawed according to package directions	10	10
Butter (or hard margarine), melted	6 tbsp.	100 mL
Cooked long grain white rice (about 1 cup, 250 mL, uncooked)	3 cups	750 mL

Filling: Heat first amount of cooking oil in large frying pan or Dutch oven on medium. Add chicken. Scramble-fry for about 10 minutes until no longer pink. Drain. Transfer to medium bowl. Cover to keep warm.

Heat second amount of cooking oil in same frying pan. Add next 7 ingredients. Cook for 5 to 10 minutes, stirring often, until onion is softened and liquid is evaporated.

Add flour. Heat and stir for 1 minute.

Slowly add broth, stirring constantly. Heat and stir until boiling and thickened.

Add next 3 ingredients and chicken. Stir.

Pie: Work with 1 pastry sheet at a time. Keep remaining sheets covered with a damp towel to prevent drying. Brush 1 side of sheet with melted butter. Fold into thirds lengthwise to make 4 inch (10 cm) wide strip. Place across centre of greased 9 inch (22 cm) springform pan, allowing ends of strip to hang over edge. Brush second pastry sheet with melted butter. Fold into thirds lengthwise. Lay over first pastry strip at an angle, slightly overlapping. Repeat with 3 more pastry sheets and butter until entire pan is covered. Gently press pastry to fit in pan, forming shell.

Press half of rice firmly in bottom of pastry shell. Spread half of chicken mixture evenly over rice. Brush remaining pastry sheets with butter and fold into thirds lengthwise. Cover filling, overlapping at an angle to make a second layer. Layer remaining rice and chicken mixture over pastry. Fold overhanging pastry over filling toward centre of pie. Filling will not be completely covered. Brush pastry with melted butter. Bake in 350°F (175°C) oven for about 90 minutes until pastry is crisp and golden and internal temperature reaches 160°F (70°C). Let stand for 15 minutes. Cuts into 8 wedges.

1 wedge: 487 Calories; 26.2 g Total Fat (4.9 g Mono, 1.3 g Poly, 7.6 g Sat); 29 mg Cholesterol; 41 g Carbohydrate; 1 g Fibre; 21 g Protein; 704 mg Sodium

Pictured at left.

*Ease into your evening
with the following:*

SIDE DISHES

Spinach Strawberry
Salad, page 121

Lemon Split Pea Soup,
page 118

DESSERT

Pumpkin Pecan Pound
Cake, page 154

SOME LIKE IT HOT

Do you have friends who live life on the edge, are the first to try new things and like their food to pack a spicy punch? This seafood-laden linguine spiked with vodka and jalapeño is the perfect dish to serve them. If you follow the rest of our menu suggestions, your friends will get to sample three other dishes that artfully weave in different types of chili peppers—each with varying intensities of heat.

SIMPLIFY: Instead of making the Chili Raspberry Vinaigrette, use 1/2 cup (125 mL) of store-bought raspberry vinaigrette and add 1/4 tsp. (1 mL) of dried crushed chilies.

Instead of preparing the Chili Tapenade Toast, simply serve store-bought garlic bread.

DRINK SUGGESTION: Bring the chili pepper theme full circle and serve chilled chili-infused martinis before dinner.

Chili Vodka Linguine With Shrimp

Not your average cream sauce! We've spiked this seafood-laden pasta with vodka and jalapeños for a spicy bite you won't soon forget.

Water	12 cups	3 L
Salt	1 1/2 tsp.	7 mL
Linguine	12 oz.	340 g
Olive oil	1 tsp.	5 mL
Finely chopped prosciutto (or deli) ham	1/3 cup	75 mL
Garlic cloves, minced (or 1/2 tsp., 2 mL powder)	2	2
Half-and-half cream	2 cups	500 mL
Vodka	1/2 cup	125 mL
Butter	2 tbsp.	30 mL
Finely chopped canned sliced jalapeño pepper, drained (see Tip, page 101)	1 tbsp.	15 mL
Salt	1/2 tsp.	2 mL
Pepper	1/4 tsp.	1 mL
Small bay scallops	1/2 lb.	225 g
Uncooked medium shrimp (peeled and deveined)	1/2 lb.	225 g
Lemon juice	1 tbsp.	15 mL
Chopped fresh parsley	1 tbsp.	15 mL

Combine water and salt in Dutch oven. Bring to a boil. Add pasta. Boil, uncovered, for 10 to 12 minutes, stirring occasionally, until tender but firm. Drain. Return to same pot. Cover to keep warm.

Heat olive oil in large frying pan on medium. Add ham and garlic. Heat and stir for about 2 minutes until fragrant.

Add next 6 ingredients. Stir. Simmer, uncovered, for 8 to 10 minutes, stirring occasionally, until slightly thickened.

Add scallops and shrimp. Stir. Cook for 3 to 5 minutes until shrimp turn pink and scallops are opaque. Remove from heat.

Stir in lemon juice. Add to pasta. Toss until coated. Transfer to large serving platter. Sprinkle with parsley. Makes about 8 cups (2 L). Serves 4.

1 serving: 736 Calories; 25.0 g Total Fat (7.2 g Mono, 1.5 g Poly, 13.7 g Sat); 178 mg Cholesterol; 72 g Carbohydrate; 3 g Fibre; 40 g Protein; 591 mg Sodium

Pictured at left.

CHILI WINE LINGUINE WITH SHRIMP: Use same amount of dry (or alcohol-free) white wine instead of vodka.

For a truly chili pepper-inspired evening, we suggest including:

SIDE DISHES

Chili Raspberry Greens, page 131

Chili Tapenade Toasts, page 135

DESSERT

Sweet Chili Fruit Galette, page 148

Chili Tapenade Toasts

Sweet Chili Fruit Galette

Left: Grilled Salmon With Mango Chutney
Right: Curried Wild Rice Pilaf

MAPLE MAGNIFICENCE

What better way to welcome out-of-country guests to the taste of Canadian cooking than with a meal inspired by our greatest-known export, maple syrup! With the addition of Canadian hospitality, this meal is guaranteed to be a success. Your feature entree is a barbecued, maple-glazed salmon served with a perfectly complementary mango and pear chutney.

SIMPLIFY: Instead of making the dip, buy a pre-made dip or mix sour cream with some dry onion soup mix.

Steam some frozen mixed veggies in place of the Grilled Balsamic Vegetables.

Instead of making the pilaf, purchase a pasta or grain salad from your favourite deli.

Grilled Salmon With Mango Chutney

Mild, tender salmon and spicy chutney are a dynamic duo that will make your next dinner party simply super.

MANGO PEAR CHUTNEY

Sesame (or cooking) oil	1 tsp.	5 mL
Finely chopped red onion	1 cup	250 mL
Garlic clove, minced (or 1/4 tsp., 1 mL, powder)	1	1
Apple cider vinegar	1/4 cup	60 mL
Maple (or maple-flavoured) syrup	1/4 cup	60 mL
Brown sugar, packed	2 tbsp.	30 mL
Finely grated gingerroot	2 tsp.	10 mL
Dried crushed chilies	1/4 tsp.	1 mL
Salt	1/4 tsp.	1 mL
Pepper	1/8 tsp.	0.5 mL
Coarsely chopped frozen mango pieces	3 cups	750 mL
Diced peeled pear	2 cups	500 mL

SALMON

Salmon fillets (4 – 5 oz., 113 – 140 g, each), skin removed	8	8
Cooking oil	2 tsp.	10 mL
Salt	1 tsp.	5 mL
Pepper	1/2 tsp.	2 mL

Mango Pear Chutney: Heat sesame oil in medium saucepan on medium. Add onion and garlic. Cook, uncovered, for 5 to 10 minutes, stirring often, until onion is softened.

Add next 7 ingredients. Cook, uncovered, for 5 minutes, stirring occasionally, to blend flavours.

Add mango and pear. Stir. Bring to a boil on medium. Simmer, uncovered, for 5 to 8 minutes, stirring occasionally, until fruit is softened. Makes about 3 1/2 cups (875 mL) chutney.

Salmon: Brush fillets with cooking oil. Sprinkle with salt and pepper. Preheat gas barbecue to medium-high. Cook salmon on greased grill for 3 to 5 minutes per side until fish flakes easily when tested with fork. Serve with Mango Pear Chutney. Serves 8.

1 serving: 333 Calories; 13.8 g Total Fat (6.1 g Mono, 3.0 g Poly, 3.1 g Sat); 75 mg Cholesterol; 30 g Carbohydrate; 3 g Fibre; 23 g Protein; 424 mg Sodium

Pictured on page 7 and at left.

To give your entire menu the Canadian treatment, we suggest:

APPETIZER
Clam And Bacon Dip, page 71

SIDE DISHES
Grilled Balsamic Vegetables, page 117

Curried Wild Rice Pilaf, page 102

DESSERT
Maple Rum Pears, page 163

BEVERAGE
Orange Maple Iced Tea, page 91

Curried Wild Rice Pilaf

Grilled Balsamic Vegetables

Maple Rum Pears

MAKE-AHEAD FLAMENCO FIESTA

Considering Spain's colourful history, outgoing and dramatic people and renowned hospitality, it's little wonder that Spanish food is so vibrant and full of life. We picture this meal served outdoors on a patio or deck with plenty of space to socialize. To ensure an atmosphere that is comfortable and casual, we've chosen recipes that can mostly be made ahead of time. The feature entree is a delightful Mixed Spanish Grill with chicken, chorizo, shrimp and mussels.

SIMPLIFY: To give yourself a little more time, consider a tapas tray with roasted almonds, sardines and deli-bought items in place of the Roasted Red Pepper Dip, or wrap melon cubes in salami slices.

DECORATING IDEA: Mini lights around your patio will make the night sparkle. Little clay pots filled with fragrant herbs like rosemary can also make lovely centrepieces.

APPETIZER

Roasted Red Pepper Dip,
page 77

SIDE DISH

Paella Primavera,
page 121

DESSERT

Peach Melba Gels,
page 167

BEVERAGE

Citrus Splash,
page 91

*Fire up your guests for an
evening of Spanish flair
with the following:*

Mixed Spanish Grill

*Consider grilling for your next dinner party. There's sure to be something for
everyone when there's sausage, seafood and chicken on the barbecue!*

Olive oil	1/2 cup	125 mL
Dry (or alcohol-free) white wine	1/3 cup	75 mL
Lemon juice	1/4 cup	60 mL
Chopped fresh oregano	1 tbsp.	15 mL
(or 3/4 tsp., 4 mL, dried)		
Garlic cloves, minced	3	3
(or 3/4 tsp., 4 mL, powder)		
Grated orange zest	1 tbsp.	15 mL
Chopped fresh rosemary	2 tsp.	10 mL
(or 1/2 tsp., 2 mL dried, crushed)		
Paprika	1 tsp.	5 mL
Boneless, skinless chicken thighs	6	6
(about 3 oz., 85 g, each)		
Uncooked extra-large shrimp	12	12
(peeled and deveined)		
Mussels	1 lb.	454 g
Water	1/4 cup	60 mL
Chorizo (or hot Italian) sausages	3	3
(about 13 oz., 370 g)		

Combine first 8 ingredients in small bowl.

Put chicken and shrimp into large resealable freezer bag. Add 2/3 cup (150 mL) olive oil
mixture. Seal bag. Toss until coated. Let stand in refrigerator for 1 hour, turning once. Reserve
remaining olive oil mixture.

Put mussels into large bowl. Lightly tap to close any that are opened 1/4 inch (6 mm) or more.
Discard any that do not close (see Note). Arrange mussels in single layer in 9 inch (22 cm) foil
pie plate. Add water and 1/4 cup (60 mL) reserved olive oil mixture. Cover with foil.

Preheat gas barbecue to medium. Cook sausages on greased grill for about 15 minutes,
turning occasionally and brushing with reserved olive oil mixture, until browned and internal
temperature reaches 160°F (70°C). Transfer to large serving platter. Cover to keep warm.
Remove chicken from olive oil mixture. Cook chicken on greased grill for about 5 minutes
per side, brushing often with reserved olive oil mixture, until fully cooked and internal
temperature reaches 170°F (77°C). Transfer to serving platter. Cover to keep warm. Cook
mussels on ungreased grill for 8 to 10 minutes until mussels are opened. Discard any unopened
mussels. Transfer mussels to serving platter. Discard cooking liquid. Cover to keep warm.
Remove shrimp from olive oil mixture. Discard any remaining olive oil mixture. Cook on
greased grill for 1 to 2 minutes per side, brushing with reserved olive oil mixture, until pink.
Transfer to platter. Cut sausages in half. Serves 6.

*1 serving: 437 Calories; 31.0 g Total Fat (16.6 g Mono, 4.4 g Poly, 7.6 g Sat); 124 mg Cholesterol;
5 g Carbohydrate; trace Fibre; 32 g Protein; 538 mg Sodium*

Pictured at left.

Note: For safety reasons, it is important to discard any mussels that do not close before
cooking, as well as any that have not opened during cooking.

A TASTE OF THAI

Adventurous diners revel in the tastes of Thai cuisine. The complexities of the traditional flavours, such as coconut, lemon grass and the exotic spices that range from teasingly hot to fantastically fiery, give this cuisine the illusion of being difficult to make. Thai food is all about the ingredients—the methods are quite simple to follow. Your star in this showcase is a hot and spicy soup, full of crisp vegetables—quintessentially Thai!

SIMPLIFY: To make your dinner with even less fuss, buy frozen crabcakes instead and serve with Thai sweet chili sauce or substitute store-bought spring rolls for the Vegetable Wraps.

DRINK SUGGESTION: A Chinese or Thai beer like Singha would go best. Or perhaps, try a lighter Canadian beer.

Tom Yum Soup

This hot and spicy Thai specialty has complex flavours of ginger, lemongrass and lime. Reduce the amount of red chilies if you like it milder.

Prepared chicken broth	4 cups	1 L
Thinly sliced fresh shiitake mushrooms	1 cup	250 mL
Gingerroot slices (1/4 inch, 6 mm thick)	3	3
Lemon grass, bulbs only (roots and stalks removed)	3	3
Uncooked medium shrimp (peeled and deveined)	3/4 lb.	340 g
Can of shoestring-style bamboo shoots, drained	8 oz.	227 mL
Thai hot chili peppers, chopped (see Tip, page 101)	3	3
Lime juice	3 tbsp.	50 mL
Fish sauce	2 tbsp.	30 mL
Chopped fresh cilantro	2 tsp.	10 mL

Measure broth into large saucepan. Bring to a boil. Reduce heat to medium. Add mushrooms and gingerroot. Simmer, uncovered, for about 5 minutes until mushrooms are tender.

Pound lemon grass bulbs with mallet or rolling pin until partially crushed. Add to broth mixture. Add next 3 ingredients. Stir. Simmer, uncovered, for about 2 minutes until shrimp turn pink. Remove from heat. Remove and discard gingerroot and lemon grass.

Add remaining 3 ingredients. Stir. Makes about 5 cups (1.25 L). Serves 4.

1 serving: 151 Calories; 2.9 g Total Fat (0.6 g Mono, 1.1 g Poly, 0.6 g Sat); 129 mg Cholesterol; 10 g Carbohydrate; 2 g Fibre; 21 g Protein; 2302 mg Sodium

Pictured at left.

To make sure your guests get the complete Thai experience, we suggest:

APPETIZERS

Crabcakes With Sweet Garlic Sauce, page 87

Chicken Satay With Peanut Sauce, page 79

SIDE DISH

Asian Vegetable Wraps, page 101

DESSERT

Coconut Lime Tart, page 149

Crabcakes With Sweet Garlic Sauce

Asian Vegetable Wraps

Chicken Satay With Peanut Sauce

CAJUN CAROUSING

Turn the evening into a Louisiana-style affair with our Cajun-Baked Snapper. Brimming with spice, this dinner can be served any time of year. Do it up fancy and plate individual servings just like top-notch chefs do. If you like, you can prepare the soup, rice, salad and dessert ahead of time. Whatever you choose, these recipes will make for a spirited evening!

SIMPLIFY: Instead of Lemon Rhubarb Sour Cream Pie, make the rhubarb mixture and serve it over ice cream or cake.

MUSIC SUGGESTION: Real Cajun dance music like that of the Cajun Playboys or anything zydeco.

DRINK SUGGESTION: You've got to match the spice of the fish, so a medium-bodied or dry white wine like Sauvignon Blanc or Chardonnay works well.

SERVES 4

Cajun-Baked Snapper

Treat your guests to a taste of New Orleans with fish fillets in a spicy, crisp crumb coating.

Paprika	1 1/2 tsp.	7 mL
Cayenne pepper	1/2 tsp.	2 mL
Dried oregano	1/2 tsp.	2 mL
Dried thyme	1/2 tsp.	2 mL
Garlic powder	1/2 tsp.	2 mL
Onion powder	1/2 tsp.	2 mL
Salt	1/2 tsp.	2 mL
Pepper	1/2 tsp.	2 mL
Milk	1/2 cup	125 mL
Dijon mustard	1 tbsp.	15 mL
White vinegar	1 tsp.	5 mL
Snapper fillets, any small bones removed (about 6 oz., 170 g, each)	4	4
Fine dry bread crumbs	1/4 cup	60 mL
Yellow cornmeal	1/4 cup	60 mL
Butter (or hard margarine), melted	2 tbsp.	30 mL

Combine first 8 ingredients in small bowl.

Whisk next 3 ingredients and 2 tsp. (10 mL) spice mixture in small bowl. Pour into shallow baking dish or pie plate. Add fillets. Turn to coat. Let stand for 10 minutes, turning once.

Combine remaining 3 ingredients and remaining spice mixture in separate small bowl. Remove fillets from milk mixture, allowing excess to drip off. Discard any remaining milk mixture. Arrange fillets in single layer on greased baking sheet. Spread about 3 tbsp. (50 mL) crumb mixture evenly over each fillet. Broil on centre rack in oven for 6 to 8 minutes until fish flakes easily when tested with fork. Serves 4.

1 serving: 299 Calories; 9.0 g Total Fat (2.2 g Mono, 1.2 g Poly, 4.4 g Sat); 80 mg Cholesterol; 15 g Carbohydrate; 1 g Fibre; 38 g Protein; 566 mg Sodium

Pictured at left.

Get your guests' taste buds in gear with the following:

SIDE DISHES

DESSERT

Raspberry Greens

Nutty Mushroom Wild Rice

Lemon Rhubarb Sour Cream Pie

THE HIGH LIFE

An elegant dinner is never about the cost of the ingredients or the quality of china your dinner is served on. It's about presentation and making the most of the ingredients you have. Set a decadent scene with a creamy baked seafood risotto that's very rich in taste.

SIMPLIFY: For a faster setup, use precooked shrimp, canned lobster meat and/or clams instead of cooking the seafood mix for the Baked Seafood Risotto.

The Mocha Latte can be replaced by regular coffee or little cups of hot chocolate with the addition of coffee-flavoured liqueur.

DRINK SUGGESTION: A dry white wine will complement the richness of the risotto. Serve a sparkling wine or dessert wine with the tiramisu.

Baked Seafood Risotto

Imagine how impressed your guests will be when you present them with this rich, creamy risotto resplendent with the aromas of wine, seafood and lemon—and only you will know that there was no extra stirring required.

Prepared chicken broth	5 cups	1.25 L
Olive oil	2 tsp.	10 mL
Chopped red onion	2 cups	500 mL
Garlic cloves, minced (or 1/2 tsp., 2 mL, powder)	2	2
Arborio rice	2 cups	500 mL
Diced red pepper	2 cups	500 mL
Dry (or alcohol-free) white wine	1/2 cup	125 mL
Dried basil	1 tsp.	5 mL
Dried oregano	1/2 tsp.	2 mL
Salt	1/2 tsp.	2 mL
Pepper	1/2 tsp.	2 mL
Dry (or alcohol-free) white wine	1 cup	250 mL
Prepared chicken broth	1/2 cup	125 mL
Butter (or hard margarine)	1 tbsp.	15 mL
Cod fillets, any small bones removed, cut into 1 inch (2.5 cm) pieces	3/4 lb.	340 g
Packages of frozen mixed seafood, thawed (12 1/2 oz., 340 g, each)	2	2
Lemon juice	2 tbsp.	30 mL
Grated lemon zest	1 tsp.	5 mL
Chopped fresh parsley	2 tbsp.	30 mL

Measure first amount of broth into small saucepan. Bring to a boil. Reduce heat to low. Cover to keep hot.

Heat olive oil in large frying pan on medium. Add onion and garlic. Cook for 5 to 10 minutes, stirring often, until onion is softened.

Add next 7 ingredients. Heat and stir for about 1 minute until liquid is almost evaporated. Spread evenly in greased 9 x 13 inch (22 x 33 cm) baking dish. Pour hot broth over top. Cover tightly with foil. Bake in 400°F (205°F) oven for about 30 minutes until rice is almost tender. Remove foil. Stir for 2 to 3 minutes until rice mixture is creamy and liquid is almost absorbed. Let stand, covered, for 5 minutes.

Combine next 3 ingredients in large saucepan. Bring to a boil. Reduce heat to medium. Add fish and mixed seafood. Cook, uncovered, for 2 to 3 minutes until fish flakes easily when tested with fork. Drain and discard cooking liquid. Add to rice mixture. Stir.

Add lemon juice and lemon zest. Stir. Sprinkle with parsley. Makes about 10 cups (2.5 L). Serves 6.

1 serving: 303 Calories; 3.6 g Total Fat (1.6 g Mono, 1.0 g Poly, 0.8 g Sat); 175 mg Cholesterol; 36 g Carbohydrate; 2 g Fibre; 29 g Protein; 1724 mg Sodium

Pictured at left.

Variation: Use shrimp and scallop mix instead of mixed seafood.

To complete this elegant feast, we suggest:

APPETIZER

Antipasto Platter, page 75

SIDE DISHES

Walnut And Pear Salad, page 114

Peas And Bacon, page 126

DESSERT

White Chocolate Lemon Tiramisu, page 159

BEVERAGE

Mocha Latte, page 95

PUB NIGHT

Turn ordinary fish and chips into something more upscale—something your guests would swim across the pond for. This recipe takes a pub favourite to a more modern level. The heaviness often associated with fish and chips is replaced with a crisp lightness for a dressed-up, more adult version.

SIMPLIFY: Cook up some ready-made French fries in place of the potato crisps.

Instead of making Herbed Tortillas, buy tortilla or pita chips to serve with the soup.

DRINK SUGGESTION: There is no better drink to go with fish and chips than beer!

Panko Fish And Crisps With Chili Tartar Sauce

A modern take on traditional fish and chips. Panko crumbs are Japanese bread crumbs that create a wonderfully crunchy coating for these fish fillets. You'll find them in the Asian foods aisle at your grocery store or in Asian supermarkets.

CHILI TARTAR SAUCE

Mayonnaise	1/3 cup	75 mL
Dijon mustard	2 tsp.	10 mL
Finely chopped dill pickle	2 tsp.	10 mL
Lime juice	2 tsp.	10 mL
Finely chopped chipotle peppers in adobo sauce (see Tip, page 125)	1/2 tsp.	2 mL

POTATO CRISPS

Grated baking potato	1 1/2 cups	375 mL
Grated orange-fleshed sweet potato	1 1/2 cups	375 mL
Large egg, fork-beaten	1	1
Garlic powder	1/4 tsp.	1 mL
Salt	1/2 tsp.	2 mL
Pepper	1/4 tsp.	1 mL
Cooking oil	2 tbsp.	30 mL

PANKO-CRUSTED FISH

All-purpose flour	1/4 cup	60 mL
Seasoned salt	1/4 tsp.	1 mL
Large eggs, fork-beaten	2	2
Panko crumbs	1/2 cup	125 mL
Dried crushed chilies	1/4 tsp.	1 mL
Seasoned salt	1/2 tsp.	2 mL
Pepper	1/4 tsp.	1 mL
Haddock fillets, any small bones removed (4 – 5 oz., 113 – 140 g, each)	4	4
Cooking spray		

Chili Tartar Sauce: Whisk all 5 ingredients in small bowl until combined. Chill, covered. Makes about 1/2 cup (125 mL) sauce.

Potato Crisps: Place potato and sweet potato in tea towel. Twist towel to remove excess moisture. Transfer to small bowl.

Add next 4 ingredients. Stir well.

Heat 1 tbsp. (15 mL) cooking oil in large frying pan on medium. Use 1/4 cup (60 mL) measure to drop 4 mounds of potato mixture into pan. Flatten into 4 inch (10 cm) diameter circles. Cook for about 3 minutes per side until browned and crisp. Transfer to greased baking sheet. Repeat with remaining cooking oil and potato mixture. Set aside.

Panko-Crusted Fish: Combine flour and first amount of seasoned salt on large plate.

Beat eggs in large shallow bowl.

Combine next 4 ingredients on separate large plate.

Pat fillets dry with paper towels. Press both sides of fillets into flour mixture. Dip into egg mixture. Press both sides of fillets into panko mixture until coated. Discard any remaining flour, egg and panko mixtures. Arrange fillets on greased baking sheet. Spray with cooking spray. Place potato crisps on bottom rack in oven. Broil fillets on top rack in oven for about 5 minutes until fish flakes easily when tested with fork and crisps are heated through. Serve with Chili Tartar Sauce. Serves 4.

1 serving: 614 Calories; 22.6 g Total Fat (11.5 g Mono, 6.5 g Poly, 2.8 g Sat); 251 mg Cholesterol; 55 g Carbohydrate; 4 g Fibre; 46 g Protein; 1037 mg Sodium

Pictured at left.

Modernize your pub grub with the following:

SIDE DISHES

Tomato Salad With Orange Basil Dressing, page 122

Chilled Pea Dill Soup With Herbed Tortillas, page 97

DESSERT

Brandied Cherry Brownies, page 145

DEEP PURPLE

Purple, most often used to symbolize royal stature, is the perfect thematic colour for a sumptuous meatless feast. Often people feel that a meal without meat may be lacking—show your guests that just isn't so. Our feature entree is a very clever take on the notion of an "egg roll." Thick strips of eggplant (also known as aubergine) are rolled around a decadent filling of cream cheese, walnuts and sun-dried

SIMPLIFY: Instead of making the appetizers, put together a platter with grapes and a variety of cheeses.

Instead of preparing the risotto, use a store-bought risotto or instant rice mix.

DRINK SUGGESTION: A lighter-bodied wine such as a Sémillon or a Chenin Blanc would be the perfect complement to this

Eggplant Rolls

Who says you need meat to make an elegant main course? Roll eggplant strips around a sinfully creamy and tangy filling for a supper that will wow meat-eaters and vegetarians alike.

Medium eggplants (about 3/4 lb., 340 g, each)	4	4
Water	10 cups	2.5 L
Salt	1 tsp.	5 mL
Block of cream cheese, softened	8 oz.	250 g
Jar of roasted red peppers, drained and chopped	12 oz.	340 g
Crumbled feta cheese	2/3 cup	150 mL
Fine dry bread crumbs	1/2 cup	125 mL
Sun-dried tomatoes in oil, blotted dry and chopped	1/2 cup	125 mL
Chopped walnuts, toasted (see Tip, page 79)	2 tbsp.	30 mL
Cooking oil	2 tsp.	10 mL
Chopped onion	1 cup	250 mL
Garlic cloves, minced (or 1/2 tsp., 2 mL, powder)	2	2
Dried oregano	1 tsp.	5 mL
Pepper	1/2 tsp.	2 mL
Tomato pasta sauce	1 cup	250 mL
Tomato pasta sauce	1 cup	250 mL
Half-and-half cream	1 cup	250 mL
Chopped walnuts, toasted (see Tip, page 79)	2 tbsp.	30 mL
Chopped fresh parsley	1 tbsp.	15 mL

Slice about 1/4 inch (6 mm) from ends of eggplants. Discard ends. Cut each eggplant lengthwise into five 1/4 inch (6 mm) slices. Combine water and salt in Dutch oven or large pot. Bring to a boil. Cook eggplant slices, covered, in 3 batches. Transfer to 2 paper towel-lined baking sheets. Press with paper towels to remove excess moisture. Set aside.

Mash cream cheese with fork in large bowl. Add next 5 ingredients. Mix well.

Heat cooking oil in medium frying pan on medium. Add onion. Cook for 5 to 10 minutes, stirring often, until softened.

Add next 3 ingredients. Heat and stir for about 1 minute until fragrant. Add to cream cheese mixture. Stir.

Spoon first amount of pasta sauce into greased 9 x 13 inch (22 x 33 cm) baking dish. Lay eggplant slices on work surface. Spread about 2 1/2 tbsp. (37 mL) cream cheese mixture over each eggplant slice. Roll up, jelly-roll style. Place seam-side down over pasta sauce in baking dish.

Combine second amount of pasta sauce and cream in small bowl. Pour over rolls. Bake, uncovered, in 375°F (190°C) oven for about 45 minutes until hot and bubbling. Let stand for 10 minutes.

Sprinkle with second amount of walnuts and parsley. Serves 10.

1 serving: 333 Calories; 18.9 g Total Fat (5.7 g Mono, 3.0 g Poly, 9.1 g Sat); 43 mg Cholesterol; 32 g Carbohydrate; 6 g Fibre; 9 g Protein; 886 mg Sodium

Pictured at left.

To present a truly royal spread, we suggest:

APPETIZERS

Vegetable Spread, page 83

Blue Cheese Toasts, page 71

SIDE DISH

Spinach Risotto, page 111

DESSERT

Mocha Tarts, page 157

IT'S SHOWTIME!

Lights! Camera! Action! Gather your friends and head for the movies. This easy, interactive evening is fun from the get-go. Nosh on do-it-yourself pizzas that your guests can make to their own specifications. Then head on into the TV room for a night of movie-watching mania.

SIMPLIFY: Forgo the fondue and simply serve veggies and dip.

Instead of making the bark and the popcorn, substitute your favourite movie-watching snacks. Or better yet, make plain popcorn and provide your guests with a variety of seasonings to try.

DECORATING IDEA: Because you're going to be watching movies, make sure your guests are comfortable. Have a selection of comfy pillows at the ready.

DIY Pizza

A whole new twist on the popular pizza party—do-it-yourself pizza. You make the crust and supply the toppings and your guests make their own creations.

Warm water	2 cups	500 mL
Granulated sugar	1 tbsp.	15 mL
All-purpose flour	3 1/2 cups	875 mL
Cake flour	2 cups	500 mL
Envelope of instant yeast	1/4 oz.	8 g
(or 2 1/4 tsp., 11 mL)		
Salt	1 tbsp.	15 mL
Yellow cornmeal, approximately	1/4 cup	60 mL

Stir water and sugar in small bowl until sugar is dissolved.

Put next 4 ingredients into food processor. Process for about 5 seconds until combined. With motor running, slowly add water mixture through hole in feed chute. Process for 1 to 2 minutes until dough forms a sticky ball that pulls away from sides of bowl. Turn out dough onto lightly floured surface. Knead for about 1 minute until smooth and elastic. Divide into 6 equal portions. Place portions on greased large baking sheet, turning once to grease tops. Wrap baking sheet with plastic wrap. Let stand in refrigerator for 1 hour or until needed. Punch dough down.

Sprinkle 1 tsp. (5 mL) cornmeal on work surface. Roll out 1 ball of dough to 6 inch (15 cm) circle. Repeat with remaining cornmeal and dough. Layer toppings of choice on dough (see Variations). Heat ungreased large baking sheet in 500°F (260°C) oven until hot. Sprinkle baking sheet with 1 to 2 tsp. (5 to 10 mL) cornmeal. Transfer 2 to 3 pizzas to greased baking sheet, using 2 spatulas. Bake on bottom rack for about 12 minutes until crust is golden and cheese is melted. Repeat with remaining pizzas. Makes 6 pizzas.

1 pizza (crust only): 398 Calories; 0.5 g Total Fat (0.1 g Mono, 0.2 g Poly, 0.1 g Sat); 0 mg Cholesterol; 87 g Carbohydrate; 2 g Fibre; 11 g Protein; 1172 mg Sodium

VEGETARIAN PIZZA: Use tomato sauce. For toppings, use fresh tomatoes, mushrooms, peppers, onion, and your favourite cheese.

SOUTHWESTERN PIZZA: Use salsa for pizza sauce. For toppings, use artichoke hearts, black beans, Mexican cheese blend or jalapeño Monterey Jack cheese.

GREEK PIZZA: Use tomato sauce. For toppings, use olives, fresh spinach leaves, green pepper and feta cheese.

ITALIAN PIZZA: Use pasta or pizza sauce. Add basil pesto to the sauce for more flavour. For toppings, use sun-dried tomatoes, Italian-style cold cuts, cooked Italian sausage, mozzarella cheese and fresh basil. Pictured at left.

ASIAN PIZZA: Use teriyaki or peanut sauce. For toppings, use cooked chicken, green onion, bean sprouts, red pepper, grated carrots, sesame seeds and mozzarella cheese.

Pictured at left and on page 169.

To make your pizza night a real award winner, we suggest:

APPETIZER

DESSERTS

BEVERAGE

Buttery Toffee Popcorn

Tiger Butter Bark

GO WITH THE GRAIN

There are times when you and your guests may feel like trying a vegetarian dinner. A good place to start is with a dish featuring a tasty, popular grain—quinoa (KEEN-wah). When your guests take a bite of this dish, they won't miss the meat at all.

SIMPLIFY: Serve a store-bought savoury cracker instead of making Cheddar Crisps.

A store-bought carrot cake or cake mix could be substituted for the Chocolate Carrot Cake.

DECORATING IDEA: Use funky, upbeat dinnerware with environmentally friendly placemats, napkins and table coverings.

Vegetable Quinoa Pie

A nutty oat crust holds vegetables in a curry-flavoured custard and our new favourite grain—quinoa (KEEN-wah). One bite and it's sure to be your favourite, too!

NUT CRUST		
Quick-cooking rolled oats	1 1/2 cups	375 mL
All-purpose flour	1 cup	250 mL
Butter (or hard margarine), softened	1/2 cup	125 mL
Finely chopped unsalted mixed nuts, toasted (see Tip, page 79)	1/2 cup	125 mL
Brown sugar, packed	2 tbsp.	30 mL
VEGETABLE PIE		
Prepared vegetable broth	1 cup	250 mL
Salt	1/8 tsp.	0.5 mL
Quinoa, rinsed and drained	2/3 cup	150 mL
Cooking oil	2 tsp.	10 mL
Chopped fresh white mushrooms	3 cups	750 mL
Chopped onion	2 cups	500 mL
Garlic cloves, minced (or 1/2 tsp., 2 mL, powder)	2	2
Chopped cauliflower	3 cups	750 mL
Chopped red pepper	1 cup	250 mL
Grated carrot	1 cup	250 mL
All-purpose flour	2 tbsp.	30 mL
Curry powder	2 tsp.	10 mL
Salt	1/2 tsp.	2 mL
Pepper	1/4 tsp.	1 mL
Grated Gruyère cheese	1 cup	250 mL
Grated sharp Cheddar cheese	1 cup	250 mL
Large eggs	6	6
Milk	2 cups	500 mL

Nut Crust: Mix all 5 ingredients in medium bowl until mixture resembles coarse crumbs. Press firmly into bottom and halfway up sides of greased 3 quart (3 L) shallow baking dish. Bake in 350°F (175°C) oven for about 15 minutes until just golden. Let stand on wire rack to cool.

Vegetable Pie: Combine broth and salt in small saucepan. Bring to a boil. Add quinoa. Stir. Reduce heat to medium-low. Simmer, covered, for about 20 minutes, without stirring, until quinoa is tender and liquid is absorbed. Fluff with fork. Transfer to large bowl.

Heat cooking oil in large frying pan on medium. Add next 3 ingredients. Cook for about 10 minutes, stirring often, until onion is softened.

Add next 3 ingredients. Stir. Sprinkle with next 4 ingredients. Heat and stir for 1 minute. Add to quinoa. Stir. Let stand for 10 minutes.

Add Gruyère and Cheddar cheese. Stir.

Whisk eggs and milk in medium bowl until combined. Add to quinoa mixture. Stir. Pour into Nut Crust. Spread evenly. Bake for about 1 hour until knife inserted in centre comes out clean and top is golden. Let stand for 10 minutes. Cuts into 6 pieces.

1 piece: 787 Calories; 43.4 g Total Fat (14.8 g Mono, 4.1 g Poly, 20.1 g Sat); 271 mg Cholesterol; 71 g Carbohydrate; 8 g Fibre; 32 g Protein; 751 mg Sodium

Pictured at left.

Make your meatless meal magnificent with the following:

APPETIZER
Cheddar Crisps, page 80

SIDE DISHES
Chipotle Red Pepper Soup, page 125

Honey Lime Sourdough Salad, page 141

DESSERT
Chocolate Carrot Cake, page 161

AN EVENING OF RED AND GOLD

In traditional Chinese culture, red and gold are the colours of celebration. Whether it be Chinese New Year, a wedding or any other joyous celebration, these colours are bound to dominate. So, what better way to celebrate the culture than with these vibrant colours and a modern take on the Asian-inspired feast? For our main dish we've chosen beautiful red-glazed pork tenderloin—we wouldn't want to clash now, would we?

SIMPLIFY: For appetizers, forgo dumplings and stuffed peppers and buy frozen dim sum of your choice. Serve with premade dipping sauces.

For an easier Veggie Chow Mein, stir-fry Oriental-style frozen veggies in oyster sauce and serve over thin, Chinese-style egg noodles.

DRINK SUGGESTION: Serve green tea with the meal for added Asian authenticity.

Easy Chinese BBQ Pork

Ever wish you could make that tasty red-glazed pork served at your favourite Chinese restaurant? Well, now you can.

Hoisin sauce	3 tbsp.	50 mL
Dry sherry	2 tbsp.	30 mL
Liquid honey	2 tbsp.	30 mL
Soy sauce	2 tbsp.	30 mL
Oyster sauce	1 tbsp.	15 mL
Chinese five-spice powder	1/4 tsp.	1 mL
Red food colouring (optional)	1/4 tsp.	1 mL
Pork tenderloins (3/4 – 1 lb., 340 – 454 g, each), trimmed of fat and halved lengthwise	2	2
Liquid honey	1 tbsp.	15 mL
Water	1 tbsp.	15 mL
Sesame oil (for flavour)	2 tsp.	10 mL
Drops of red food colouring (optional)	2	2

Combine first 7 ingredients in small bowl.

Put pork into large resealable freezer bag. Add hoisin mixture. Seal bag. Turn until coated. Let stand in refrigerator for 4 hours, turning occasionally. Transfer hoisin mixture to small saucepan. Bring to a boil. Boil, covered, for 5 minutes. Remove from heat. Place pork on greased rack in broiler pan containing about 1/2 inch (12 mm) water. Brush pork with reserved hoisin mixture. Broil on centre rack in oven for 10 minutes, turning and brushing with reserved hoisin mixture at halftime, until browned. Turn oven on to 400°F (205°C). Brush pork with hoisin mixture. Bake for 5 minutes, brushing once.

Combine remaining 4 ingredients in small dish. Brush over pork. Broil for about 5 minutes, turning and brushing at halftime with honey mixture, until dull reddish-brown colour and internal temperature reaches 160°F (71°C). Remove to cutting board. Cover with foil. Let stand for 10 minutes. Cut into thin slices. Serves 8.

1 serving: 162 Calories; 4.9 g Total Fat (2.1 g Mono, 1.0 g Poly, 1.4 g Sat); 54 mg Cholesterol; 9 g Carbohydrate; trace Fibre; 18 g Protein; 350 mg Sodium

Pictured at left.

To make the celebration complete, we suggest:

APPETIZERS
Steamed Pork Dumplings, page 84

Shrimp-Stuffed Peppers, page 72

SIDE DISH
Veggie Chow Mein, page 133

DESSERT
Sake Mellowed Melon, page 149

Shrimp-Stuffed Peppers

Sake Mellowed Melon

Steamed Pork Dumplings

SPRING HAS SPRUNG

The grass is getting green again, seedlings are poking their delicate stems out of the earth and birds can be heard singing their sweet songs. It's time to shed that old winter attitude and join the spring revival with all that is fresh and new. Our springtime offering is tender lamb chops with a fresh mint and parsley topping—and just an added touch of chili heat.

SIMPLIFY: Instead of making the Salmon Pastry Puffs, make the salmon filling, adding 3 oz. (85 g) of cream cheese, and mix well to create a salmon spread. Serve with crackers.

In place of the asparagus, serve a salad of mixed baby greens with raspberry vinaigrette.

Serve your favourite sorbet instead of making the mousse cups.

Herbed Lamb Chops

Remember green eggs and ham? How about green herbs and lamb? We've heated up the classic combo of lamb and mint with just a hint of chili.

Lamb loin chops (about 1 1/2 lbs., 680 g)	8	8
Zesty Italian dressing	1/4 cup	60 mL
FRESH HERB TOPPING		
Fresh parsley, lightly packed	1 cup	250 mL
Fresh mint, lightly packed	1/4 cup	60 mL
Olive (or cooking) oil	3 tbsp.	50 mL
Balsamic vinegar	1 tbsp.	15 mL
Garlic clove, minced	1	1
(or 1/4 tsp., 1 mL, powder)		
Dried crushed chilies	1/2 tsp.	2 mL

Put lamb chops into large resealable freezer bag. Add dressing. Seal bag. Turn until coated. Let stand in refrigerator for 2 to 3 hours, turning occasionally.

Fresh Herb Topping: Put all 6 ingredients into blender or food processor. Process until paste-like consistency. Makes about 1/4 cup (60 mL) topping. Remove lamb chops from freezer bag. Discard any remaining dressing. Place on greased broiler pan. Broil on top rack in oven for about 4 minutes per side for medium-rare or until desired doneness. Drizzle topping over lamb chops. Serves 4.

1 serving: 465 Calories; 38.5 g Total Fat (17.0 g Mono, 2.6 g Poly, 11.7 g Sat); 98 mg Cholesterol; 3 g Carbohydrate; trace Fibre; 25 g Protein; 339 mg Sodium

Pictured at left.

To maintain the bounty of freshness, we suggest:

APPETIZER
Salmon Pastry Puffs,
page 85

SIDE DISHES
Honey Basil Asparagus,
page 135
Roasted baby potatoes

DESSERT
Orange Rhubarb Mousse
Cups, page 166

BEVERAGE
Spiced Berry Splash,
page 89

Spiced Berry Splash

Salmon Pastry Puffs

Orange Rhubarb Mousse Cups

SOUTHWESTERN SUNSET

This dinner theme was inspired by life on a ranch, where the eating is simple, yet satisfying and the atmosphere is friendly and casual. By the time the stunning colours of the sunset are displayed, your guests will be relaxing with dessert and ready to spin yarns about life on the range. The feature attractions to this laid-back gathering are succulent ribs first rubbed with spices, then basted in a tangy and mildly spicy barbecue sauce.

SIMPLIFY: Instead of preparing Chili Corn, simply steam frozen corn.

Instead of Peach Lemonade, use a flavoured lemonade mix.

For dessert, forgo the crisp and serve a fruit salad of fresh blueberries and strawberries with a scoop of vanilla ice cream.

DRINK SUGGESTION: A cold beer is the perfect complement to this supper. Place mugs in the freezer first so they're frosty.

Southwestern-Style Ribs

A slow-cooked dish robust with flavour. Sure to send your barbecue dinner guests into an eating frenzy.

BARBECUE SAUCE		
Chili sauce	1/2 cup	125 mL
Liquid honey	1/4 cup	60 mL
Apple cider vinegar	1 tbsp.	15 mL
Finely chopped onion	1 tbsp.	15 mL
Dijon mustard	1 1/2 tsp.	7 mL
Worcestershire sauce	1 1/2 tsp.	7 mL
CHILI RUB		
Brown sugar, packed	1 tsp.	5 mL
Chili powder	1 tsp.	5 mL
Garlic powder	1 tsp.	5 mL
Onion powder	1 tsp.	5 mL
Paprika	1 tsp.	5 mL
Ground thyme	1/2 tsp.	2 mL
Dried rosemary, crushed	1/4 tsp.	1 mL
Salt	1/4 tsp.	1 mL
Pepper	1/4 tsp.	1 mL
RIBS		
Baby back pork ribs (about 2 racks)	2 lbs.	900 g

Barbecue Sauce: Combine all 6 ingredients in small bowl. Chill. Makes about 1 cup (250 mL) sauce.

Chili Rub: Combine all 9 ingredients in small cup. Makes about 2 tbsp. (30 mL) rub.

Ribs: Spread Chili Rub on both sides of each rack of ribs. Wrap with plastic wrap. Let stand in refrigerator for at least 2 hours. Preheat gas barbecue to medium. Remove plastic wrap from ribs. Place ribs on side of greased grill. Turn off burner under ribs, leaving opposite burner on medium. Close lid. Cook for about 60 minutes, turning occasionally, until meat is tender and just starting to pull away from bones. Brush with Barbecue Sauce. Cook for about 30 minutes, turning often and brushing with sauce, until glazed. Transfer to large plate. Cover with foil. Let stand for 10 minutes. Cut into 3 or 4 bone portions. Serves 4.

1 serving: 764 Calories; 53.7 g Total Fat (24.2 g Mono, 4.6 g Poly, 19.8 g Sat); 184 mg Cholesterol; 31 g Carbohydrate; 1 g Fibre; 37 g Protein; 1332 mg Sodium

Pictured at left.

Fill out your meal with other ranch favourites:

SIDE DISHES

Chili Corn, page 125

Coleslaw, page 134

Potato salad, bought from the local deli

DESSERT

Bumbleberry Crisp, page 147

BEVERAGE

Peach Lemonade, page 90

Peach Lemonade

Chili Corn

Bumbleberry Crisp

LEI IT ON THICK

Sometimes entertaining is way too serious. With this feast we want you to explore your fun side. Take out that tacky tiki lamp and set the stage for an evening of bright and festive tropical flavours. To begin, serve sweet and spicy glazed pork chops with a side of tangy bean sprout salad.

SIMPLIFY: Substitute canned pineapple chunks for fresh in the Hawaiian Bacon Bites.

The Coconut Custard Pie can be replaced by a citrusy or tropical-flavoured store-bought cream pie.

DRINK SUGGESTION: Serve fruity tropical drinks, with or without

Luau Pork Chops And Sprout Salad

Get set to party Hawaiian-style! These sweet and spicy glazed pork chops come with their own side—a tangy bean sprout salad with rice vinegar and nutty sesame oil.

SPROUT SALAD

Chopped green onion	1/3 cup	75 mL
Granulated sugar	1 tbsp.	15 mL
Rice vinegar	1 tbsp.	15 mL
Soy sauce	1 tbsp.	15 mL
Sesame oil (for flavour)	2 tsp.	10 mL
Sesame seeds, toasted (see Tip, page 79)	2 tsp.	10 mL
Fresh bean sprouts (about 1 lb., 454 g)	6 cups	1.5 L
Boiling water	4 cups	1 L

LUAU PORK CHOPS

Cooking oil	1 – 2 tbsp.	15 – 30 mL
Boneless pork loin chops (about 3/4 inch, 2 cm, thick, each), trimmed of fat	8	8
Liquid honey	1/3 cup	75 mL
Dry sherry	1/4 cup	60 mL
Hoisin sauce	1/4 cup	60 mL
Orange juice	1/4 cup	60 mL
Soy sauce	2 tbsp.	30 mL
Sesame oil, for flavour	1 tbsp.	15 mL
Chili paste (sambal oelek)	1 tsp.	5 mL

Sprout Salad: Combine first 6 ingredients in large bowl.

Blanch bean sprouts, uncovered, in boiling water in Dutch oven for 30 seconds. Drain. Rinse with cold water. Drain well. Add to soy sauce mixture. Toss until coated. Chill, covered, tossing occasionally. Makes about 4 cups (1 L) salad.

Luau Pork Chops: Heat 1 tbsp. (15 mL) cooking oil in large frying pan on medium-high. Cook pork in 2 batches, for about 4 minutes per batch, turning at halftime, until browned. Add remaining cooking oil between batches if necessary to prevent sticking. Transfer to plate. Cover to keep warm. Drain and discard drippings from pan. Reduce heat to medium.

Add remaining 7 ingredients to same frying pan. Stir. Bring to a boil. Cook for about 10 minutes, stirring and scraping any brown bits from bottom of pan, until thickened. Add pork chops. Cook, covered, for 1 to 2 minutes until no longer pink inside. Transfer Sprout Salad to large serving platter. Arrange pork over top. Spoon honey mixture over pork. Serves 8.

1 serving: 442 Calories; 25.4 g Total Fat (11.0 g Mono, 3.9 g Poly, 8.1 g Sat); 69 mg Cholesterol; 31 g Carbohydrate; 3 g Fibre; 24 g Protein; 500 mg Sodium

Pictured at left.

Let the hula party begin with these menu suggestions:

APPETIZER
Hawaiian Bacon Bites, page 83

SIDE DISH
Tropical Rice Salad, page 98

DESSERT
Coconut Custard Pie, page 155

THE MORE THE MERRIER

You're expecting a houseful of company and that's what you love—lots of friends and family around the table. What better to serve than a roast? But this is no ordinary piece of pork. We've dressed it up with the tart yet sweet flavours of cranberry and apple.

SIMPLIFY: For Tapenade Tomatoes, use a store-bought tapenade.

Rather than Stuffed Pasta Shells, buy a pre-made rosé sauce and serve over any cooked pasta.

No time to bake a cake from scratch? Use a chocolate cake mix, adding 1 tsp. (5 mL) finely grated orange zest to the mix.

DRINK SUGGESTION: An off-dry white wine such as Sauvignon Blanc or Sémillon Chardonnay would be the perfect drink complement.

Cranberry Apple Pork Roast

If you think cranberries are just for Thanksgiving turkey, then you must try this tender pork roast dressed up with a bright cranberry sauce spiced with ginger, jalapeño pepper and lime.

Boneless pork loin roast	4 – 4 1/2 lbs.	1.8 – 2 kg
Salt	1/4 tsp.	1 mL
Pepper	1/4 tsp.	1 mL
CRANBERRY APPLE SAUCE		
Frozen (or fresh) cranberries	3 cups	750 mL
Chopped peeled cooking apple (such as McIntosh)	2 cups	500 mL
Liquid honey	1/2 cup	125 mL
Frozen concentrated apple juice	3 tbsp.	50 mL
Chopped fresh jalapeño pepper (see Tip, page 101)	2 tbsp.	30 mL
Finely chopped gingerroot	1 tbsp.	15 mL
Grated lime zest	1 tsp.	5 mL

Place roast in large roasting pan. Sprinkle with salt and pepper. Bake, uncovered, in 400°F (205°C) oven for 30 minutes. Reduce heat to 325°F (160°C). Bake, uncovered, for about 45 minutes until meat thermometer inserted into thickest part of roast reads at least 155°F (68°C) or desired doneness. Transfer to cutting board. Cover with foil. Let stand for 10 minutes. Cut roast into thin slices. Arrange on serving platter.

Cranberry Apple Sauce: Combine all 7 ingredients in medium saucepan. Bring to a boil. Reduce heat to medium. Simmer, uncovered, for about 10 minutes, stirring occasionally, until cranberries are soft. Makes about 3 cups (750 mL) sauce. Spoon over pork. Serves 12.

1 serving: 340 Calories; 15.4 g Total Fat (6.7 g Mono, 1.4 g Poly, 5.8 g Sat); 91 mg Cholesterol; 19 g Carbohydrate; 2 g Fibre; 30 g Protein; 122 mg Sodium

Pictured at left.

For a complete full-table menu, we suggest:

APPETIZER
Tapenade Tomatoes, page 79

SIDE DISHES
Stuffed Pasta Shells, page 129

Orange-Glazed Vegetables, page 139

DESSERT
Chocolate Orange Chiffon Cake, page 167

Stuffed Pasta Shells   Orange-Glazed Vegetables   Chocolate Orange Chiffon Cake

A LITTLE SOUTHERN COMFORT

The best things take time and we've learned a thing or two from our neighbours down south. When you take life slow and easy, it's all the sweeter. Share this philosophy by serving a succulent, slow-basted whisky and molasses-glazed ham with a hint of Georgia peach.

SIMPLIFY: Mashed potatoes would do nicely in place of Slow Cooker Scallop.

No time to make squares? Serve pie filling over ice cream.

DRINK SUGGESTION: A fruity punch for the adults and an alcohol-free version of the same for kids.

DECORATING IDEA: Decorate your table with a Southern belle fan at each lady's setting and a shot glass at each man's setting.

Whisky Molasses–Glazed Ham

For impressive entrees, you can't beat a whole roasted ham, especially with a sweet, smoky and peppery glaze. Save the bone to make flavourful soup stock.

WHISKY MOLASSES GLAZE

Frozen concentrated orange juice, thawed	1/2 cup	125 mL
Peach jam	1/3 cup	75 mL
Fancy (mild) molasses	1/4 cup	60 mL
Canadian whisky (rye)	3 tbsp.	50 mL
Dijon mustard	2 tbsp.	30 mL
Coarsely ground pepper	1 1/2 tsp.	7 mL
Partially cooked skinless ham (bone-in), fat trimmed to 1/4 inch (6 mm) thick	8 – 10 lbs.	3.6 – 4.5 kg

Whiskey Molasses Glaze: Combine all 6 ingredients in small saucepan. Bring to a boil on medium. Reduce heat to medium-low. Simmer, uncovered, for about 15 minutes until thickened. Makes about 1 cup (250 mL) glaze.

Place ham in large roasting pan. Bake, covered, in 325°F (160°C) oven for about 2 hours until meat thermometer inserted in thickest part of ham reads 130°F (54°C). Brush with Whisky Molasses Glaze. Bake, uncovered, for about 1 hour, brushing with glaze every 15 minutes, until meat thermometer inserted into thickest part of ham reads 160°F (71°C). Cover with foil. Let stand for 10 minutes. Brush with pan juices. Slice ham. Serves 12.

1 serving: 393 Calories; 14.6 g Total Fat (6.9 g Mono, 1.3 g Poly, 5.1 g Sat); 145 mg Cholesterol; 15 g Carbohydrate; trace Fibre; 46 g Protein; 134 mg Sodium

Pictured at left.

To complete a meal to slowly savour, we suggest:

SIDE DISHES

Slow Cooker Scallop, page 106

Napa Apple Salad, page 107

DESSERT

Berry Dream Squares, page 161

Napa Apple Salad   Slow Cooker Scallop   Berry Dream Squares

Top Left: Lemon Garlic-Dressed Greens
Top Right: Smashed Baby Potatoes
Bottom: Honey Garlic Ginger Lamb

MIX AND MINGLE

Sometimes you want a great meal, but you don't want to sacrifice spending time with your guests. On these occasions, a dinner that allows you ample prep time is tops. That's what our Honey Garlic Ginger Lamb is all about. You'll get to show off your culinary finesse and still have time to chat.

SIMPLIFY: Rather than Lemon Garlic-Dressed Greens, serve a mixed green salad with a store-bought tangy vinaigrette.

For the Ginger Almond Trifle, use instant vanilla pudding for custard or buy a trifle from your favourite bakery.

DRINK SUGGESTION: A full-bodied Shiraz goes well with these flavourful dishes.

Honey Garlic Ginger Lamb

Want to really impress your guests? It doesn't get more impressive than a whole roasted leg of lamb. Sweet and tangy Asian spices breathe extra flavour into the tender meat.

HONEY GARLIC GINGER SAUCE		
Liquid honey	1/2 cup	125 mL
Garlic cloves, minced	3	3
(or 3/4 tsp., 4 mL, powder)		
Finely grated gingerroot	2 tbsp.	30 mL
Soy sauce	2 tbsp.	30 mL
Hoisin sauce	1 tbsp.	15 mL
Dijon mustard	2 tsp.	10 mL
Lemon juice	2 tsp.	10 mL
Sesame oil (for flavour)	2 tsp.	10 mL
ROAST LAMB		
Boneless leg of lamb roast	3 1/2 – 4 lbs.	1.6 – 1.8 kg
Small garlic cloves, halved	8	8
Salt	1 tsp.	5 mL
Pepper	1/2 tsp.	2 mL
Cooking oil	2 tbsp.	30 mL

Honey Garlic Ginger Sauce: Combine all 8 ingredients in small saucepan. Bring to a boil. Reduce heat to medium-low. Simmer, uncovered, for 5 minutes, stirring occasionally, to blend flavours. Makes about 1 cup (250 mL) sauce. Transfer 1/2 cup (125 mL) to small cup. Set aside.

Roast Lamb: Tie roast with butcher's string into uniform shape. Cut 16 small slits in roast, about 1/2 inch (12 mm) deep, using small sharp knife. Place 1 garlic half in each slit. Sprinkle with salt and pepper.

Heat cooking oil in large frying pan on medium-high. Add roast. Cook for 1 to 2 minutes per side until browned. Place roast on greased wire rack set in foil-lined medium roasting pan. Brush with sauce. Bake, uncovered, in 325°F (160°C) oven for about 1 3/4 hours until internal temperature reaches 140°F (60°C) for medium-rare or until desired doneness. Cover with foil. Let stand for 10 minutes. Cut roast into thin slices. Transfer to serving platter. Drizzle reserved Honey Garlic Ginger Sauce over top. Serves 12.

1 serving: 302 Calories; 15.3 g Total Fat (6.8 g Mono, 1.9 g Poly, 5.3 g Sat); 88 mg Cholesterol; 13 g Carbohydrate; trace Fibre; 26 g Protein; 423 mg Sodium

Pictured at left.

To maximize your mingling time, we suggest:

SIDE DISHES

Lemon Garlic-Dressed Greens, page 129

Smashed Baby Potatoes, page 137

Strawberry Cucumber Soup, page 105

DESSERT

Ginger Almond Trifle, page 151

Strawberry Cucumber Soup

Lemon Garlic-Dressed Greens

Ginger Almond Trifle

GO EASY

Let the slow cooker work its magic. Put this stew on in the morning, do a little prep work on your other menu items and you should have time to sample that Rumtini by early afternoon. Much of the preparation for this menu can be done in advance. This flavourful stew has a true East Indian twist and goes great with a loaf of crusty bread, flatbread or even in a bread bowl.

MUSIC SUGGESTION: Throw a Ravi Shankar CD into your player to create an Eastern ambience.

DECORATING IDEA: Keep it earthy and low-key with golden-hued candles and rustic shades like cayenne or curry.

Lamb And White Bean Stew

Mint is the secret ingredient that pulls together all the complex, hearty spices in this delicious lamb stew.

Sliced carrot, 1/2 inch (12 mm) thick	3 cups	750 mL
Large fennel bulb (white part only), halved and thinly sliced	1	1
Cooking oil	1 tbsp.	15 mL
Stewing lamb	1 1/2 lbs.	680 g
Cooking oil	1 tsp.	5 mL
Thinly sliced onion	2 cups	500 mL
Garlic cloves, minced (or 1/2 tsp., 2 mL, powder)	2	2
Whole green cardamom, bruised (see Tip, page 95)	4	4
Cinnamon stick (4 inches, 10 cm)	1	1
Finely grated gingerroot (or 1/2 tsp., 2 mL, ground ginger)	2 tsp.	10 mL
Salt	3/4 tsp.	4 mL
Dried crushed chilies	1/2 tsp.	2 mL
Ground cumin	1/2 tsp.	2 mL
Prepared beef broth	1 cup	250 mL
Cans of navy beans, rinsed and drained (14 oz., 398 mL, each)	2	2
Chopped fresh mint	1/4 cup	60 mL

Layer carrot and fennel, in order given, in 4 to 5 quart (4 to 5 L) slow cooker.

Heat first amount of cooking oil in large frying pan on medium-high. Add lamb. Cook for about 5 minutes, stirring occasionally, until browned. Transfer to slow cooker. Reduce heat to medium.

Add second amount of cooking oil to same frying pan. Add onion and garlic. Cook for 5 to 10 minutes, stirring often, until onion is softened.

Add next 6 ingredients. Heat and stir for 1 to 2 minutes until fragrant.

Slowly add broth, stirring constantly and scraping any brown bits from bottom of pan. Add beans. Stir. Pour over lamb. Cook, covered, on Low for 8 to 9 hours or on High for 4 to 4 1/2 hours. Remove and discard cinnamon stick and cardamom. Transfer to serving bowl.

Sprinkle with mint. Makes about 8 cups (2 L). Serves 6.

1 serving: 394 Calories; 10.0 g Total Fat (4.3 g Mono, 1.8 g Poly, 2.6 g Sat); 74 mg Cholesterol; 42 g Carbohydrate; 11 g Fibre; 35 g Protein; 1219 mg Sodium

Pictured at left.

BEEF AND WHITE BEAN STEW: Use same amount of stewing beef instead of lamb.

Take it easy with the following menu suggestions:

SIDE DISH
Bittersweet Apple Salad, page 113

DESSERT
Pear Masala Crepes, page 157

BEVERAGE
Ginger CranApple Rumtinis, page 89

Ginger CranApple Rumtinis

Pear Masala Crepes

Bumbleberry Crisp, page 147

Perfect Pairings

Rich Viennese Coffee, page 95

Blue Cheese Toasts, page 71

Blue Cheese Toasts

Let your guests indulge in fancy fare they wouldn't usually get at home. These toasted baguette slices with savoury blue cheese and sweet grape halves are sure to make your guests feel pampered.

Baguette bread slices, 1 inch (2.5 cm) thick	20	20
Olive (or cooking) oil	1 tbsp.	15 mL
Crumbled blue cheese	1/2 cup	125 mL
Seedless grapes, halved	30	30
Grated mozzarella cheese	1 1/2 cups	375 mL

Arrange baguette slices in single layer on ungreased baking sheet. Lightly brush tops with olive oil. Broil on centre rack in oven for 2 to 4 minutes until golden. Turn slices over.

Sprinkle with blue cheese. Arrange 3 grape halves over blue cheese on each toast. Sprinkle with mozzarella cheese. Broil for 1 to 2 minutes until cheese is melted. Transfer to serving plate. Serve immediately. Makes 20 toasts.

1 toast: 77 Calories; 3.7 g Total Fat (1.1 g Mono, 0.1 g Poly, 1.8 g Sat); 10 mg Cholesterol; 8 g Carbohydrate; trace Fibre; 4 g Protein; 140 mg Sodium

Pictured on page 70 and on back cover.

Clam And Bacon Dip

A little land, a little sea and you've created a smoky, creamy, mildly spicy dip to delight. Serve hot or cold with crackers, pita or tortilla chips.

Diced bacon	1 cup	250 mL
Finely chopped red onion	1 cup	250 mL
Garlic cloves, minced (or 1/2 tsp. 2 mL, powder)	2	2
Finely chopped red pepper	1/2 cup	125 mL
Block of cream cheese, softened	8 oz.	250 g
Sour cream	1/2 cup	125 mL
Lemon juice	2 tsp.	10 mL
Pepper	1/4 tsp.	1 mL
Cans of minced clams (5 oz., 142 g, each), drained	2	2
Finely chopped canned sliced jalapeño peppers (see Tip, page 101)	2 tsp.	10 mL

Heat small frying pan on medium. Add first 3 ingredients. Cook for about 10 minutes, stirring occasionally, until bacon is almost crisp.

Add red pepper. Stir. Cook for 2 to 4 minutes until red pepper is tender-crisp. Transfer with slotted spoon to paper towel-lined plate to drain. Set aside.

Beat next 4 ingredients in small bowl until light and smooth.

Add clams, jalapeños and bacon mixture. Mix well. Makes about 3 cups (750 mL).

1/4 cup (60 mL): 197 Calories; 16.3 g Total Fat (6.3 g Mono, 1.3 g Poly, 8.0 g Sat); 48 mg Cholesterol; 4 g Carbohydrate; trace Fibre; 10 g Protein; 617 mg Sodium

Pictured below.

Clam And Bacon Dip, above

Shrimp-Stuffed Peppers

Shrimp-stuffed green peppers drizzled with a mildly spicy peanut sauce add an elegant impact to any evening.

Coarsely chopped green pepper	1/4 cup	60 mL
Coarsely chopped onion	1/4 cup	60 mL
Uncooked shrimp (peeled and deveined)	3/4 lb.	340 g
Egg white (large)	1	1
Chopped fresh cilantro or parsley	2 tbsp.	30 mL
Cornstarch	2 tbsp.	30 mL
Sesame oil (for flavour)	1 tsp.	5 mL
Chili paste (sambal oelek)	1/4 tsp.	1 mL
Small green peppers	4	4
Soy sauce	1/4 cup	60 mL
Brown sugar, packed	1 tbsp.	15 mL
Smooth peanut butter	1 tbsp.	15 mL
White vinegar	1 tbsp.	15 mL
Chili paste (sambal oelek)	1/4 tsp.	1 mL

Put green pepper and onion into food processor. Process until finely chopped. Add shrimp. Process with on/off motion until chopped.

Add next 5 ingredients. Process until well mixed and thick paste consistency.

Cut green peppers into quarters. Remove seeds and ribs. Spoon about 2 tbsp. (30 mL) shrimp mixture onto each pepper piece. Place on greased baking sheet. Broil on centre rack in oven for 10 to 12 minutes until filling is browned and peppers are tender-crisp.

Combine remaining 5 ingredients in small saucepan. Heat and stir on medium for 3 to 5 minutes until boiling and sugar is dissolved. Drizzle over peppers. Makes 16 stuffed peppers.

1 stuffed pepper: 46 Calories; 1.2 g Total Fat (0.4 g Mono, 0.4 g Poly, 0.2 g Sat); 32 mg Cholesterol; 4 g Carbohydrate; trace Fibre; 5 g Protein; 237 mg Sodium

Pictured on page 53 and at left.

Shrimp-Stuffed Peppers, right

Crab And Artichoke Pâté

This lavish crab pâté offers a creamy texture with the perfectly blended flavours of artichoke, cream cheese, fresh herbs and capers. Spread on toasted baguette slices, crackers or cucumber slices.

Block of cream cheese, softened	8 oz.	250 g
Jar of marinated artichoke hearts, drained, finely chopped	6 oz.	170 mL
Can of crabmeat, drained, cartilage removed, flaked	4 1/4 oz.	120 g
Finely chopped green onion	1/3 cup	75 mL
Butter (or hard margarine), softened	1/4 cup	60 mL
Chopped fresh dill (or 1/4 tsp., 1 mL, dried)	1 tsp.	5 mL
Chopped fresh tarragon (or 1/4 tsp., 1 mL, dried)	1 tsp.	5 mL
Anchovy paste	1/2 tsp.	2 mL
Grated lemon zest	1/2 tsp.	2 mL
Capers, chopped (optional)	1 tbsp.	15 mL

Mash cream cheese with fork in medium bowl. Add remaining 9 ingredients. Mix well. Makes about 2 1/4 cups (550 mL).

2 tbsp. (30 mL): 76 Calories; 6.9 g Total Fat (1.9 g Mono, 0.3 g Poly, 4.3 g Sat); 26 mg Cholesterol; 1 g Carbohydrate; trace Fibre; 3 g Protein; 119 mg Sodium

Pictured on page 4 and below.

Crab And Artichoke Pâté, above

Cheese And Pepper Pinwheels

These curry-flavoured pinwheels offer an appealing and flavourful nibble before the main course is served. For a colourful variation, use sun-dried tomato tortillas.

Grated sharp Cheddar cheese	1 cup	250 mL
Finely chopped red pepper	1/3 cup	75 mL
Mayonnaise	1/4 cup	60 mL
Vegetable cream cheese	1/4 cup	60 mL
Finely chopped green onion	1 tbsp.	15 mL
Curry powder	1/2 tsp.	2 mL
Spinach tortillas (9 inch, 22 cm, diameter)	3	3
Shredded lettuce, lightly packed	1 cup	250 mL

Combine first 6 ingredients in small bowl.

Spread cheese mixture evenly on tortillas, leaving 3/4 inch (2 cm) edge. Sprinkle lettuce over cheese mixture. Roll up tightly, jelly-roll style. Wrap rolls with plastic wrap. Chill. Place rolls, seam-side down, on cutting board. Trim ends. Cut rolls into 8 slices each. Makes 24 pinwheels.

1 pinwheel: 58 Calories; 4.2 g Total Fat (1.1 g Mono, 0.5 g Poly, 1.8 g Sat); 8 mg Cholesterol; 3 g Carbohydrate; trace Fibre; 2 g Protein; 98 mg Sodium

Antipasto Platter, page 75

Antipasto Platter

North Americans have adopted this favourite from their Italian cousins. Antipasto literally means "before a meal" and with all the treasured tastes of Italy—artichoke, mushroom, pepper and prosciutto—your guests' appetites are sure to be primed for the main course.

BALSAMIC VINAIGRETTE

Balsamic vinegar	3 tbsp.	50 mL
Olive oil	2 tbsp.	30 mL
Finely chopped sun-dried tomatoes in oil	2 tsp.	10 mL
Dried basil	1/4 tsp.	1 mL
Garlic powder	1/4 tsp.	1 mL
Dried oregano	1/8 tsp.	0.5 mL
Salt, just a pinch		
Pepper, just a pinch		

ANTIPASTO

Small red pepper, cut into 1 1/2 inch (3.8 cm) pieces	1	1
Small yellow pepper, cut into 1 1/2 inch (3.8 cm) pieces	1	1
Large fennel bulb (white part only), cut into 1/2 inch (12 mm) wedges	1	1
Medium portobello mushrooms, quartered	3	3
Olive oil	1 tbsp.	15 mL
Salt	1/4 tsp.	1 mL
Pepper	1/8 tsp.	0.5 mL
Cherry tomatoes, halved	24	24
Can of artichoke hearts, drained	14 oz.	398 mL
Prosciutto slices (about 6 oz., 170 g)	12	12

Balsamic Vinaigrette: Combine all 8 ingredients in small cup. Makes about 1/3 cup (75 mL) vinaigrette.

Antipasto: Put first 4 ingredients into extra-large bowl. Drizzle with olive oil. Sprinkle with salt and pepper. Toss until coated. Spread evenly on baking sheet with sides. Bake in 400°F (205°C) oven for 20 minutes.

Add tomatoes. Stir. Bake for about 10 minutes until vegetables are tender and browned. Transfer to large bowl.

Add artichokes. Drizzle with Balsamic Vinaigrette. Toss until coated. Let stand for 30 minutes, stirring occasionally.

Roll up prosciutto slices. Arrange prosciutto on large platter. Arrange vegetable mixture on platter. Drizzle any remaining vinaigrette over vegetables. Serves 6.

1 serving: 198 Calories; 10.2 g Total Fat (5.1 g Mono, 0.7 g Poly, 2.0 g Sat); 22 mg Cholesterol; 16 g Carbohydrate; 3 g Fibre; 12 g Protein; 1045 mg Sodium

Pictured on pages 74 and 169.

Moroccan Chicken Fig Balls

In our humble opinion, figs, the food of Greek gods and ancient Roman nobility, are too seldom enjoyed. Give your guests a rare taste experience with flavourful little meatballs with fig centres—complete with a fresh and cool mint dipping sauce. For a sweeter variation, use dates instead.

MINT DIPPING SAUCE

Plain yogurt	1/2 cup	125 mL
Chopped fresh mint	1 tbsp.	15 mL
Grated lemon zest	1 tsp.	5 mL
Granulated sugar	1/2 tsp.	2 mL
Salt	1/4 tsp.	1 mL
Garlic powder	1/8 tsp.	0.5 mL

FIG MEATBALLS

Large egg, fork-beaten	1	1
Fine dry bread crumbs	1/4 cup	60 mL
Lemon juice	2 tsp.	10 mL
Grated lemon zest	1 tsp.	5 mL
Ground cumin	1 tsp.	5 mL
Chili paste (sambal oelek)	1/2 tsp.	2 mL
Ground cinnamon	1/4 tsp.	1 mL
Lean ground chicken	1 lb.	454 g
Dried figs, quartered	9	9

Mint Dipping Sauce: Combine all 6 ingredients in small bowl. Chill, covered. Makes about 1/2 cup (125 mL) sauce.

Fig Meatballs: Combine first 7 ingredients in large bowl.

Add chicken. Mix well. Roll into 36 balls. Dent each ball with thumb.

Place 1 fig piece in each dent. Re-roll each ball to completely cover fig. Arrange on greased baking sheet with sides. Bake in 400°F (205°C) oven for about 15 minutes until fully cooked and internal temperature reaches 175°F (80°C). Serve with Mint Dipping Sauce. Makes 36 meatballs.

1 meatball with 3/4 tsp. (4 mL) sauce: 46 Calories; 2.1 g Total Fat (0.1 g Mono, 0.1 g Poly, 0.2 g Sat); 6 mg Cholesterol; 4 g Carbohydrate; 1 g Fibre; 3 g Protein; 36 mg Sodium

Citrus Shrimp Salad Ceviche, right

Citrus Shrimp Salad Ceviche

This fresh mixture of peppers, shrimp, tomato and avocado is reminiscent of the kind of food you would get when enjoying fine dining—certainly a treat and certainly tantalizing! If you like, substitute minced chipotle pepper for the chili powder. Serve with tortilla chips.

Uncooked medium shrimp (peeled and deveined)	1 lb.	454 g
Finely chopped green pepper	1/4 cup	60 mL
Finely chopped orange (or red) pepper	1/4 cup	60 mL
Cooking oil	3 tbsp.	50 mL
Finely chopped onion	3 tbsp.	50 mL
Lemon juice	2 tbsp.	30 mL
Lime juice	2 tbsp.	30 mL
Orange juice	2 tbsp.	30 mL
Finely chopped jalapeño pepper (see Tip, page 101)	1 tbsp.	15 mL
Chili powder	1/2 tsp.	2 mL
Salt	1/2 tsp.	2 mL
Pepper	1/4 tsp.	1 mL
Diced avocado	3/4 cup	175 mL
Diced fresh tomato	3/4 cup	175 mL
Chopped fresh cilantro	1/4 cup	60 mL

Pour water into large saucepan. Bring to a boil. Add shrimp. Cook, uncovered, for about 1 minute until starting to turn pink. Drain. Plunge into ice water in large bowl. Let stand until cool. Drain. Coarsely chop shrimp.

Combine next 11 ingredients in medium bowl. Add shrimp. Toss. Chill, covered, for 1 hour to blend flavours.

Add remaining 3 ingredients. Toss gently. Makes about 4 3/4 cups (1.2 L).

1/2 cup (125 mL): 117 Calories; 7.0 g Total Fat (3.8 g Mono, 1.9 g Poly, 0.7 g Sat); 73 mg Cholesterol; 4 g Carbohydrate; 1 g Fibre; 10 g Protein; 197 mg Sodium

Pictured at left.

Roasted Red Pepper Dip

This homey red pepper dip is made unique with the clever addition of sherry vinegar and fresh rosemary. Spoon onto baguette slices or pair with spicy sausage, meatballs, cheese or garlic-laced baby potatoes.

Olive oil	2 tbsp.	30 mL
Finely chopped onion	1/3 cup	75 mL
Garlic cloves, minced (or 3/4 tsp., 4 mL powder)	3	3
Dried crushed chilies	1/2 tsp.	2 mL
Can of navy beans, rinsed and drained	14 oz.	398 mL
Roasted red peppers	1 1/2 cups	375 mL
Tomato paste	2 tbsp.	30 mL
Sherry vinegar (see Note)	1 tbsp.	15 mL
Chopped fresh rosemary (or 1/4 tsp., 1 mL, dried, crushed), optional	1 tsp.	5 mL
Salt	1/4 tsp.	1 mL
Chopped fresh parsley (or 3/4 tsp., 4 mL, flakes)	1 tbsp.	15 mL

Heat olive oil in small frying pan on medium. Add next 3 ingredients. Cook for about 5 minutes, stirring often, until onion is softened.

Put next 6 ingredients into food processor. Add onion mixture. Process with on/off motion until almost smooth. Transfer to shallow medium bowl.

Sprinkle with parsley. Cool to room temperature. Makes about 3 cups (750 mL).

1/2 cup (125 mL): 160 Calories; 5.6 g Total Fat (3.4 g Mono, 0.5 g Poly, 0.7 g Sat); 0 mg Cholesterol; 22 g Carbohydrate; 6 g Fibre; 6 g Protein; 633 mg Sodium

Pictured below.

Note: Sherry vinegar adds a nice Spanish authenticity, but white wine vinegar could be used instead.

Roasted Red Pepper Dip, above

Baked Chèvre Crostini

Whipping cream and goat cheese are richly rewarding for your taste buds. Elegant to look at and delicious to eat.

BASIL VINAIGRETTE		
Fresh basil, lightly packed	1/2 cup	125 mL
Olive oil	1/4 cup	60 mL
Balsamic vinegar	2 tbsp.	30 mL
Liquid honey	1 tbsp.	15 mL
Salt, just a pinch		
Pepper, just a pinch		
CROSTINI		
Baguette bread slices, 1/2 inch (12 mm) thick	20	20
Olive oil	2 tbsp.	30 mL
Goat (chèvre) cheese, room temperature	9 oz.	250 g
Whipping cream	1/2 cup	125 mL
Chopped fresh basil	1 tsp.	5 mL
Strips of roasted red pepper	20	20
Chopped fresh basil	1/4 cup	60 mL

Basil Vinaigrette: Put all 6 ingredients into blender or food processor. Process until smooth. Makes about 1/3 cup (75 mL) vinaigrette.

Crostini: Lightly brush both sides of baguette slices with olive oil. Arrange on ungreased baking sheet. Broil on centre rack in oven for 2 to 3 minutes, turning once, until golden.

Combine next 3 ingredients in small bowl. Spread about 1 tbsp. (15 mL) on each baguette slice.

Arrange red pepper over top. Broil on top rack in oven for 1 to 2 minutes until bubbling.

Sprinkle with basil. Drizzle with Basil Vinaigrette. Serve immediately. Makes 20 crostini.

1 crostini: 127 Calories; 9.2 g Total Fat (4.2 g Mono, 0.5 g Poly, 3.7 g Sat); 15 mg Cholesterol; 8 g Carbohydrate; trace Fibre; 4 g Protein; 118 mg Sodium

Chicken Satay With Peanut Sauce, page 79

Chicken Satay
With Peanut Sauce

Skewers of chicken satay have always been a favourite at Thai restaurants. Bring your guests a little of that authentic flavour paired with a delectable peanut sauce.

Boneless, skinless chicken breast halves	1 lb.	454 g
Sesame oil (for flavour)	2 tbsp.	30 mL
Paprika	1/2 tsp.	2 mL
Salt	1 tsp.	5 mL
Pepper	1/2 tsp.	2 mL
Bamboo skewers (8 inches, 20 cm, each), soaked in water for 10 minutes	12	12
PEANUT SAUCE		
Sesame oil (for flavour)	1/2 tsp.	2 mL
Finely grated gingerroot	2 tsp.	10 mL
Garlic cloves, minced (or 1/2 tsp., 2 mL, powder)	2	2
Peanut butter	1/3 cup	75 mL
Brown sugar, packed	2 tbsp.	30 mL
Lime juice	2 tbsp.	30 mL
Soy sauce	2 tbsp.	30 mL
Chili paste (sambal oelek)	1/2 tsp.	2 mL
Light coconut milk	1/2 cup	125 mL

Cut each chicken breast into 4 or 5 strips, about 1/2 inch (12 mm) wide. Put into large resealable freezer bag. Combine next 4 ingredients in small cup. Pour over chicken. Seal bag. Toss until coated. Let stand in refrigerator for 1 to 2 hours, turning occasionally. Remove chicken. Discard any remaining sesame oil mixture.

Thread chicken accordion-style onto skewers. Arrange on baking sheet, lined with greased foil. Bake in 350°F (175°C) oven for about 15 minutes, turning at halftime, until no longer pink inside.

Peanut Sauce: Heat sesame oil in small saucepan on medium. Add gingerroot and garlic. Heat and stir for about 1 minute until fragrant. Add next 5 ingredients. Heat and stir for about 5 minutes until peanut butter is melted.

Add coconut milk. Heat and stir for about 1 minute until bubbling. Cool to room temperature. Makes about 1 cup (250 mL) sauce. Serve with Chicken Skewers. Makes 12 skewers.

1 skewer with 4 tsp. (20 mL) sauce: 125 Calories; 7.3 g Total Fat (2.9 g Mono, 2.1 g Poly, 1.7 g Sat); 22 mg Cholesterol; 5 g Carbohydrate; trace Fibre; 11 g Protein; 356 mg Sodium

Pictured on pages 39 and 78.

Tip: When toasting nuts, seeds or coconut, cooking times will vary for each type of nut—so never toast them together. For small amounts, place ingredient in an ungreased frying pan. Heat on medium for 3 to 5 minutes, stirring often, until golden. For larger amounts, spread ingredient evenly in an ungreased baking sheet with sides. Bake in a 350°F (175°C) oven for 5 to 10 minutes, stirring or shaking often, until golden.

Tapenade Tomatoes, below

Tapenade
Tomatoes

Tapenade is an olive lover's dream come true. Here we've slathered it on fresh tomatoes and sprinkled it with fresh basil. Fresh vine-ripened tomatoes are the best choice for this dish.

BLACK OLIVE TAPENADE		
Olive oil	1/3 cup	75 mL
Balsamic vinegar	2 tbsp.	30 mL
Pine nuts, toasted (see Tip, this page)	2 tbsp.	30 mL
Anchovy paste	1 tsp.	5 mL
Garlic cloves, minced (or 1/4 tsp., 1 mL, powder)	1 tsp.	5 mL
Pitted kalamata olives	2 cups	500 mL
TOMATOES		
Large ripe tomatoes	6	6
Chopped fresh basil	1/4 cup	60 mL

Black Olive Tapenade: Put first 5 ingredients into blender or food processor. Process until smooth.

Add olives. Process with on/off motion until olives are coarsely chopped. Makes about 1 3/4 cups (425 mL) tapenade.

Tomatoes: Cut thin slice from bottom and top of each tomato. Discard ends. Cut tomatoes in half horizontally. Arrange in single layer in large shallow serving dish. Spoon tapenade over tomatoes.

Sprinkle with basil. Makes 12 tomatoes.

1 tomato: 150 Calories; 13.9 g Total Fat (4.8 g Mono, 1.0 g Poly, 1.0 g Sat); trace Cholesterol; 7 g Carbohydrate; 1 g Fibre; 1 g Protein; 368 mg Sodium

Pictured above.

Cheddar Crisps

With a little cumin and chili powder, these cheddar crisps have just the right amount of sharpness and heat. They can be enjoyed as is or served as dippers.

Butter (or hard margarine), softened	1/3 cup	75 mL
Granulated sugar	1 tbsp.	15 mL
Large egg	1	1
All-purpose flour	1 cup	250 mL
Finely grated sharp Cheddar cheese	1 cup	250 mL
Chili powder	1/4 tsp.	1 mL
Ground cumin	1/4 tsp.	1 mL
Salt	1/4 tsp.	1 mL
Pepper	1/4 tsp.	1 mL

Cream butter and sugar in medium bowl. Add egg. Beat well.

Combine remaining 6 ingredients in small bowl. Add to butter mixture. Stir. Knead until no dry flour remains and soft dough forms. Form into 8 inch (20 cm) long log. Wrap with plastic wrap. Freeze for about 1 hour until firm. Cut into 1/4 inch (6 mm) thick slices. Arrange on parchment (not waxed) paper-lined cookie sheet. Bake in 400°F (205°C) oven for 10 to 12 minutes until golden. Let stand on cookie sheet for 5 minutes. Remove crisps from cookie sheet and place on wire rack to cool. Makes about 32 crisps.

1 crisp: 47 Calories; 3.2 g Total Fat (0.9 g Mono, 0.1 g Poly, 2.0 g Sat); 15 mg Cholesterol; 3 g Carbohydrate; trace Fibre; 1 g Protein; 56 mg Sodium

Pictured at left and on page 125.

Cheddar Crisps, right

Feta Artichoke Mini Pockets

Filled with tangy artichoke and bold feta with a tinge of heat, these pockets may be miniature but they have a big gourmet taste. Save the marinade from the artichoke hearts to use in salad dressing.

Crumbled feta cheese	1 cup	250 mL
Jar of marinated artichoke hearts, drained	6 oz.	170 mL
Finely chopped English cucumber with peel	1/3 cup	75 mL
Mayonnaise	2 tbsp.	30 mL
Finely chopped jalapeño pepper (see Tip, page 101)	1 tbsp.	15 mL
Garlic clove, minced (or 1/4 tsp., 1 mL, powder)	1	1
Chopped fresh oregano (or 1/2 tsp., 2 mL, dried)	2 tsp.	10 mL
Pita breads (3 inch, 7.5 cm diameter), halved and opened	12	12
Whole pitted kalamata olives, for garnish		
Cherry (or grape) tomatoes, for garnish		

Put first 7 ingredients into blender or food processor. Process until almost smooth.

Spoon about 1 tbsp. (15 mL) artichoke mixture into each pita pocket. Arrange pitas on serving plate.

Garnish with olives and tomatoes. Makes 24 pockets.

1 pocket: 109 Calories; 2.3 g Total Fat (0.7 g Mono, 0.4 g Poly, 1.1 g Sat); 6 mg Cholesterol; 18 g Carbohydrate; 1 g Fibre; 4 g Protein; 258 mg Sodium

Pictured above.

Spiced Cheese Straws

These delicate buttery and spicy pastry straws will put the common bread stick to shame. For less heat, reduce chilies or use coarsely ground black pepper instead.

Package of puff pastry (14 oz., 397 g), thawed according to package directions	1/2	1/2
Butter (or hard margarine), melted	1/4 cup	60 mL
Finely grated jalapeño Monterey Jack cheese	1 cup	250 mL
Dried crushed chilies	2 tsp.	10 mL

Roll out pastry on lightly floured surface to 8 x 12 inch (20 x 30 cm) rectangle.

Brush with butter. Sprinkle with cheese and chilies. Press down lightly. Using sharp knife, cut crosswise into twenty-four 1/2 inch (12 mm) wide strips. Loosely twist strips. Arrange on parchment (not waxed) paper-lined baking sheet. Bake in 400°F (205°C) oven for about 10 minutes until golden and puffed. Makes 24 straws.

1 straw: 79 Calories; 6.6 g Total Fat (2.3 g Mono, 0.5 g Poly, 2.8 g Sat); 9 mg Cholesterol; 4 g Carbohydrate; trace Fibre; 2 g Protein; 66 mg Sodium

Hawaiian Bacon Bites, page 83

Hawaiian Bacon Bites

These sweet, smoky little bites of bacon-wrapped pineapple will be hard to resist. For convenience and ease, use precooked bacon slices.

Precooked bacon slices (see Note), halved	14	14
Fresh pineapple cubes (1/2 inch, 12 mm)	28	28
Pineapple juice	1/3 cup	75 mL
Brown sugar, packed	2 tbsp.	30 mL
Cooking oil	2 tbsp.	30 mL
Lemon juice	1 tbsp.	15 mL
Lemon pepper	1/2 tsp.	2 mL
Paprika	1/2 tsp.	2 mL
Salt	1/2 tsp.	2 mL

Wrap 1 bacon slice around each pineapple chunk. Secure with wooden pick. Arrange in single layer on pie plate.

Combine remaining 7 ingredients in small bowl. Pour over bites. Let stand, covered, in refrigerator for 1 hour. Arrange bacon bites on greased baking sheet with sides. Bake in 450°F (230°C) oven for 5 to 10 minutes until bacon is browned and crisp. Makes 28 bites.

1 bite: 38 Calories; 2.8 g Total Fat (1.4 g Mono, 0.4 g Poly, 0.9 g Sat); 6 mg Cholesterol; 1 g Carbohydrate; trace Fibre; 2 g Protein; 140 mg Sodium

Pictured on page 82.

Note: If you want to cook your own bacon slices instead of using commercially prepared bacon, remove from heat before they get crisp.

Vegetable Spread

Eggplant and sweet roasted red peppers give this dip its distinct appeal. Serve with crackers, Melba toast or pita chips.

Olive (or cooking) oil	2 tbsp.	30 mL
Chopped eggplant (with peel)	4 cups	1 L
Chopped onion	2 cups	500 mL
Garlic cloves, minced, (or 1 tsp., 5 mL, powder)	4	4
Chopped roasted red peppers	1 cup	250 mL
Balsamic vinegar	2 tbsp.	30 mL
Tomato paste	2 tbsp.	30 mL
Salt	1/2 tsp.	2 mL
Pepper	1/2 tsp.	2 mL

Heat olive oil in medium frying pan on medium. Add eggplant and onion. Cook for about 10 minutes, stirring often, until eggplant and onion are softened.

Add garlic. Heat and stir for about 1 minute until fragrant. Transfer to food processor.

Add next 5 ingredients. Process until smooth. Transfer to medium bowl. Let stand at room temperature until cool. Chill, covered, until cold. Makes about 3 cups (750 mL).

2 tbsp. (30 mL): 33 Calories; 1.1 g Total Fat (0.8 g Mono, 0.1 g Poly, 0.2 g Sat); 0 mg Cholesterol; 4 g Carbohydrate; 1 g Fibre; 1 g Protein; 142 mg Sodium

Pictured below.

Vegetable Spread, above

Steamed Pork Dumplings, right

Steamed Pork Dumplings

These homemade dumplings are an intriguing beginning to any Asian-inspired dinner.

Chopped fresh bean sprouts	1/2 cup	125 mL
Canned, sliced water chestnuts, drained and chopped	1/2 cup	125 mL
Finely chopped green onion	1 tbsp.	15 mL
Finely grated carrot	1 tbsp.	15 mL
Cornstarch	2 tsp.	10 mL
Hoisin sauce	2 tsp.	10 mL
Soy sauce	2 tsp.	10 mL
Finely grated gingerroot (or 1/4 tsp., 1 mL, ground ginger)	1 tsp.	5 mL
Sesame oil (for flavour)	1 tsp.	5 mL
Lean ground pork	1/2 lb.	225 g
Round dumpling wrappers	16	16
Water		

Combine first 9 ingredients in large bowl.

Add pork. Mix well. Roll into 16 balls, using about 1 1/2 tbsp. (25 mL) for each.

Place 1 ball in centre of each dumpling wrapper. Dampen edges of wrappers with water. Gather up wrappers around filling, pinching to make small pleats and leaving top slightly open. Tap dumplings gently on work surface to flatten bottom slightly. Arrange dumplings, evenly spaced apart, in parchment paper (or foil) lined 9 x 9 inch (22 x 22 cm) baking dish, being careful they do not touch sides of pan. Place wire rack in bottom of large roasting pan. Pour water into roasting pan until 1 inch (2.5 cm) deep. Bring to a boil on stove-top. Set baking dish on wire rack. Cook, covered, for about 15 minutes until pork mixture is no longer pink. Makes 16 dumplings.

1 dumpling: 70 Calories; 3.4 g Total Fat (1.5 g Mono, 0.4 g Poly, 1.2 g Sat); 10 mg Cholesterol; 7 g Carbohydrate; trace Fibre; 4 g Protein; 87 mg Sodium

Pictured on page 53 and at left.

Salmon Pastry Puffs

Smoked salmon always adds a touch of sophistication—and when it's combined with goat cheese, dill and green onion in puff pastry, it makes for a deliciously decadent delight.

Soft goat (chèvre) cheese	3 oz.	85 g
Finely chopped smoked salmon (about 1 1/2 oz., 43 g)	1/4 cup	60 mL
Chopped fresh dill (or 1/4 tsp., 1 mL, dried)	1 tsp.	5 mL
Finely chopped green onion	1 tsp.	5 mL
Grated lemon zest	1/2 tsp.	2 mL
Package of puff pastry (14 oz., 397 g), thawed according to package directions	1/2	1/2
Large egg, fork-beaten	1	1
Grated Parmesan cheese	1 tbsp.	15 mL

Combine first 5 ingredients in small bowl.

Roll out pastry on lightly floured surface to 10 x 7 1/2 inch (25 x 19 cm) rectangle. Cut into twelve 2 1/2 inch (6.4 cm) squares. Spoon about 2 tsp. (10 mL) goat cheese mixture onto centre of each square. Brush edges of squares with egg. Bring opposite corners together to form triangle. Press edges together to seal. Arrange about 1/2 inch (12 mm) apart on greased baking sheet. Brush tops with egg.

Sprinkle with cheese. Cut 2 or 3 small slits in top of each triangle to allow steam to escape. Bake in 400°F (205°C) oven for about 15 minutes until golden. Makes 12 puffs.

1 puff: 122 Calories; 8.5 g Total Fat (4.2 g Mono, 0.9 g Poly, 2.9 g Sat); 20 mg Cholesterol; 8 g Carbohydrate; trace Fibre; 4 g Protein; 102 mg Sodium

Pictured on page 55 and below.

Shrimply Marvellous Grillers

Grilled shrimp skewers are made magnificent with a marinade of lemon, garlic, soy and chili. An easy and unbeatable appetizer.

Lemon juice	1/4 cup	60 mL
Sesame (or cooking) oil	2 tbsp.	30 mL
Soy sauce	2 tbsp.	30 mL
Garlic powder	2 tsp.	10 mL
Onion powder	2 tsp.	10 mL
Chili paste (sambal oelek)	1 tsp.	5 mL
Uncooked large shrimp (peeled and deveined)	1 lb.	454 g
Bamboo skewers (8 inches, 20 cm, each), soaked in water for 10 minutes	6	6

Combine first 6 ingredients in ungreased 9 x 13 inch (22 x 33 cm) baking dish.

Thread shrimp onto skewers. Place in lemon juice mixture, turning to coat. Let stand, covered, in refrigerator for 30 minutes. Remove shrimp. Discard any remaining lemon juice mixture. Preheat gas barbecue to medium-high. Cook shrimp on greased grill for about 2 minutes per side until shrimp turn pink. Makes 6 skewers.

1 skewer: 97 Calories; 2.8 g Total Fat (0.8 g Mono, 1.1 g Poly, 0.5 g Sat); 115 mg Cholesterol; 2 g Carbohydrate; trace Fibre; 16 g Protein; 205 mg Sodium

Salmon Pastry Puffs, above

Crabcakes With Sweet Garlic Sauce, page 87

Crabcakes With Sweet Garlic Sauce

Baked to a golden brown, these unique crabcakes have the distinctive additions of ginger, celery and green onion. To complete the taste experience, we've also added a lively dipping sauce.

Lemon Butter Fondue, below

SWEET GARLIC SAUCE		
Granulated sugar	1/2 cup	125 mL
Water	1/4 cup	60 mL
White vinegar	1/4 cup	60 mL
Garlic cloves, minced	3	3
Chili paste (sambal oelek)	1/4 tsp.	1 mL
CRABCAKES		
Sesame (or cooking) oil	1/2 tsp.	2 mL
Finely chopped celery	1/3 cup	75 mL
Finely grated gingerroot	1 tsp.	5 mL
Finely chopped green onion	1/4 cup	60 mL
Cans of crabmeat, drained, cartilage removed, flaked (4 1/4 oz., 120 g, each)	2	2
Fine dry bread crumbs	1/3 cup	75 mL
Mayonnaise	1/4 cup	60 mL
Lime zest	1 tsp.	5 mL
Soy sauce	1 tsp.	5 mL
Pepper	1/4 tsp.	1 mL
Sesame oil (for flavour)	2 tsp.	10 mL

Sweet Garlic Sauce: Combine all 5 ingredients in small saucepan. Bring to a boil. Boil, uncovered, for about 5 minutes, stirring occasionally, until mixture is thickened. Makes about 1/2 cup (125 mL) sauce.

Crabcakes: Heat first amount of sesame oil in small frying pan on medium. Add celery and gingerroot. Cook for about 5 minutes, stirring occasionally, until celery starts to soften.

Add green onion. Heat and stir for 1 minute. Transfer to plate. Let stand for 5 minutes.

Combine next 6 ingredients in medium bowl. Add celery mixture. Stir. Divide into 12 equal portions. Shape into 1/2 inch (12 mm) thick patties. Arrange on greased baking sheet.

Brush tops with second amount of sesame oil. Bake in 375°F (190°C) oven for about 10 minutes per side until golden and heated through. Serve with Sweet Garlic Sauce. Makes 12 crabcakes.

1 crabcake with 2 tsp. (10 mL) sauce: 92 Calories; 3.7 g Total Fat (1.8 g Mono, 1.2 g Poly, 0.3 g Sat); 1 mg Cholesterol; 11 g Carbohydrate; trace Fibre; 3 g Protein; 225 mg Sodium

Pictured on pages 39 and 86.

Tip: *Steam vegetables (broccoli florets, cauliflower florets, baby carrots, green beans, sugar snap peas) individually in steamer basket over boiling water until tender-crisp. Cool quickly in ice water to preserve colour and prevent further cooking. Arrange on 2 small plates or put each vegetable into a separate bowl. Plan on 6 – 8 veggie dippers per person.*

Lemon Butter Fondue

Let your guests indulge in some fondue fun with a lemon butter sauce laced with traces of ginger and garlic. Goes well with tender-crisp steamed veggies (see Tip, this page).

Prepared chicken broth	4 cups	1 L
Dry (or alcohol-free) white wine	1/2 cup	125 mL
Lemon juice	1/4 cup	60 mL
Granulated sugar	2 tsp.	10 mL
Finely grated gingerroot (or 1/2 tsp., 2 mL, ground ginger)	2 tsp.	10 mL
Garlic clove, minced, (or 1/4 tsp., 1 mL powder)	1	1
Water	2 tbsp.	30 mL
Cornstarch	3 tbsp.	50 mL
Butter	2 tbsp.	30 mL
Lemon slices, for garnish		

Combine first 6 ingredients in medium saucepan. Bring to a boil. Reduce heat to medium. Boil gently, uncovered, for 10 to 15 minutes, stirring occasionally, until mixture is slightly reduced.

Stir water into cornstarch in small cup. Add to broth mixture. Heat and stir until boiling and thickened. Remove from heat. Add butter, 1 tbsp. (15 mL) at a time, stirring constantly, until combined. Transfer to fondue pot.

Garnish with lemon slices. Keep warm over low flame. Makes about 3 cups (750 mL).

1/4 cup (60 mL): 43 Calories; 2.3 g Total Fat (0.6 g Mono, 0.2 g Poly, 1.3 g Sat); 5 mg Cholesterol; 4 g Carbohydrate; trace Fibre; 1 g Protein; 509 mg Sodium

Pictured above.

Fruity Sangria, page 89

Spiced Berry Splash, below

Ginger CranApple Rumtini, below

Fruity Sangria

A traditional red-wine sangria is always a welcome sight at any gathering.

Bottle of sparkling apple cider (with alcohol)	12 oz.	341 mL
Orange liqueur	1/2 cup	125 mL
Medium orange, sliced	1	1
Medium lemon, sliced	1	1
Granulated sugar	2 tbsp.	30 mL
Cinnamon sticks (4 inches, 10 cm, each)	2	2
Bottle of dry red wine	25 oz.	750 mL
Diced fresh strawberries	1 cup	250 mL
Diced unpeeled tart cooking apple (such as Granny Smith)	1 cup	250 mL
Club soda, chilled	1 cup	250 mL
Lemon-lime soda, chilled	1 cup	250 mL
Ice cubes	24	24

Stir first 6 ingredients in large pitcher or small punch bowl until sugar is dissolved. Let stand, covered, for 1 hour. Squeeze and discard orange and lemon slices.

Add next 3 ingredients. Stir.

Just before serving, add remaining 3 ingredients. Stir gently. Makes about 8 1/2 cups (2.1 L).

1 cup (250 mL): 170 Calories; 0.1 g Total Fat (trace Mono, 0.1 g Poly, trace Sat); 0 mg Cholesterol; 19 g Carbohydrate; 1 g Fibre; trace Protein; 14 mg Sodium

Pictured on page 88.

Spiced Berry Splash

Spiced rum adds panache to this cool cranberry cocktail. Served in martini glasses, it's made extra special with a cinnamon and sugar-coated rim.

Cranberry cocktail	2 cups	500 mL
Can of club soda	12 1/2 oz.	355 mL
Spiced rum	1/3 cup	75 mL
Strawberry flavouring syrup	1/4 cup	60 mL
Granulated sugar	1/4 cup	60 mL
Ground cinnamon	1 tsp.	5 mL
Cranberry cocktail	2 tbsp.	30 mL
Crushed ice		

Combine first 4 ingredients in small pitcher. Stir. Makes about 4 cups (1 L).

Combine sugar and cinnamon on plate.

Pour second amount of cranberry cocktail onto separate plate. Dip rims of 8 martini glasses into cranberry cocktail. Press rims into sugar mixture until coated.

Put crushed ice into prepared glasses. Pour cocktail mixture over ice. Serves 8.

1 serving: 94 Calories; 0 g Total Fat (0 g Mono, 0 g Poly, 0 g Sat); 0 mg Cholesterol; 19 g Carbohydrate; trace Fibre; trace Protein; 14 mg Sodium

Pictured on page 55 and above.

Ginger CranApple Rumtinis

This cool creation may be reminiscent of your favourite hot Christmas toddy, but serving it chilled in a martini glass finessed with a skewer of crystallized ginger will bring good cheer any time of the year.

Sparkling apple cider (with alcohol)	4 cups	1 L
Cranberry cocktail	1 1/2 cups	375 mL
Dark rum	1/4 cup	60 mL
Gingerroot slices, about 1/4 inch (6 mm) thick (optional)	6	6
Pieces of crystallized ginger (optional)	6	6

Combine first 3 ingredients in large pitcher.

Place gingerroot slices between 2 pieces of plastic wrap. Lightly pound with mallet or rolling pin. Add to cider mixture. Stir. Chill for 2 hours. Remove and discard gingerroot. Pour mixture into 6 chilled martini glasses.

Thread crystallized ginger onto cocktail picks. Place 1 pick in each glass. Makes about 5 1/2 cups (1.4 L). Serves 6.

1 serving: 116 Calories; 0 g Total Fat (0 g Mono, 0 g Poly, 0 g Sat); 0 mg Cholesterol; 15 g Carbohydrate; trace Fibre; 0 g Protein; 2 mg Sodium

Pictured on page 67, above and on back cover.

Peach Lemonade

The tartness of lemonade is tempered with the fresh and summery taste of peaches in this sweet, yet balanced mocktail. Follow the variation for an adults-only twist.

Can of sliced peaches 14 oz. (with syrup)		398 mL
Water	3 cups	750 mL
Lemon juice	1 cup	250 mL
Granulated sugar	1/2 cup	125 mL

Put peaches and syrup into blender or food processor. Process until smooth. Remove 1 cup (250 mL) peach purée. Set aside. Fill ice cube tray with remaining peach purée. Freeze until firm.

Combine remaining 3 ingredients in large pitcher. Add reserved peach purée. Stir. Just before serving, add frozen peach purée. Stir. Makes about 5 cups (1.25 L).

1 cup (250 mL): 122 Calories; trace Total Fat (trace Mono, trace Poly, 0 g Sat); 0 mg Cholesterol; 33 g Carbohydrate; 1 g Fibre; 1 g Protein; 4 mg Sodium

Pictured on page 57 and at left.

Variation: Add 1 oz. (30 mL) white rum or peach schnapps to individual servings.

Peach Lemonade, right

Orange Maple Iced Tea, below

Pink Pineapple Refresher, below

Citrus Splash, below

Orange Maple Iced Tea

This unique iced tea is sure to make every guest feel extra-special. Serve over ice.

Boiling water	4 cups	1 L
Orange pekoe tea bags	5	5
Orange juice	4 cups	1 L
Maple (or maple-flavoured) syrup	1/2 cup	125 mL
Lemon juice	2 tbsp.	30 mL
Large orange	1	1

Pour boiling water over tea bags in tea pot. Let steep, covered, for 5 minutes. Squeeze and discard tea bags.

Combine next 3 ingredients in large pitcher. Add tea. Stir.

Cut orange into thin slices. Discard ends. Add to tea mixture. Stir. Chill, covered, until cold. Makes about 8 cups (2 L).

1 cup (250 mL): 107 Calories; 0.4 g Total Fat (0.1 g Mono, 0.1 g Poly, trace Sat); 0 mg Cholesterol; 26 g Carbohydrate; trace Fibre; 1 g Protein; 3 mg Sodium

Pictured above.

Pink Pineapple Refresher

Give your guests the delicious feeling of being pampered at an island resort with this cool, fun and frothy concoction of coconut, pineapple and orange.

Crushed ice	2 cups	500 mL
Raspberry juice, chilled	2 cups	500 mL
Piña Colada drink mix, chilled	1 cup	250 mL
Frozen concentrated pineapple-orange juice (about half of 12 1/2 oz., 355 mL, can)	6 oz.	170 mL
Orange liqueur, chilled	1/2 cup	125 mL
Club soda, chilled	2 cups	500 mL
Lemon-lime soda, chilled	2 cups	500 mL

Stir first 5 ingredients in large bowl or punch bowl until concentrated pineapple juice is thawed.

Add club and lemon-lime soda. Stir gently. Makes about 8 cups (2 L).

1 cup (250 mL): 164 Calories; 0.5 g Total Fat (trace Mono, trace Poly, 0.5 g Sat); 0 mg Cholesterol; 35 g Carbohydrate; trace Fibre; 1 g Protein; 20 mg Sodium

Pictured above and on page 169.

Citrus Splash

This über-chic take on white wine sangria is full of fresh fruit and mild spices. And if you prefer a little fizz with your festivities, add a splash of lemon-lime or club soda. Use a sweet white wine such as Gewurztztraminer for the best results. Serve with ice cubes.

Bottle of sweet (or alcohol-free) white wine	27 oz.	750 mL
Orange juice	2 cups	500 mL
Medium lemon thinly sliced	1	1
Medium orange thinly sliced	1	1
Red grapes, halved	1/2 cup	125 mL
Peach schnapps	1/4 cup	60 mL
Granulated sugar	2 tbsp.	30 mL
Spiced rum	2 tbsp.	30 mL
Cinnamon stick (4 inches, 10 cm)	1	1

Combine all 9 ingredients in large pitcher. Chill, covered, until cold. Pour liquid into 6 tall glasses. Using tongs, transfer fruit to glasses. Makes about 7 cups (1.75 L). Serves 6.

1 serving: 216 Calories; 0.3 g Total Fat (trace Mono, 0.1 g Poly, trace Sat); 0 mg Cholesterol; 26 g Carbohydrate; 1 g Fibre; 1 g Protein; 9 mg Sodium

Pictured above.

Mojitos, page 93

Kir Royale, below

Sparkling Pomegranate, below

Mojitos

Mojitos (pronounced moh-HEE-tohs) add a dash of Cuban flair with their popular lime and mint flavours.

White (light) rum	1 1/2 cups	375 mL
Lime juice	3/4 cup	175 mL
Icing (confectioner's) sugar	1/2 cup	125 mL
Club soda	2 1/2 cups	625 mL
Sprigs of fresh mint	6	6
Ice cubes	12	12

Measure first 3 ingredients into large pitcher. Stir until sugar is dissolved. Add club soda. Stir gently.

Place 1 mint sprig in each of 6 tall glasses. Crush mint with back of spoon. Add 2 ice cubes to each glass. Pour lime mixture into prepared glasses. Makes about 4 3/4 cups (1.2 L). Serves 6.

1 serving: 176 Calories; trace Total Fat (trace Mono, trace Poly, trace Sat); 0 mg Cholesterol; 13 g Carbohydrate; trace Fibre; trace Protein; 1 mg Sodium

Pictured on page 92.

Kir Royale

Give your guests the royal treatment with this retro-chic champagne cocktail. For a different spin, try other liqueurs like apricot, cherry or blackcurrant.

Bottles of sparkling white wine (or champagne), 25 1/2 oz. (750 mL) each, chilled	2	2
Raspberry liqueur	1 1/4 cups	300 mL

Pour about 2/3 cup (150 mL) sparkling wine into each of 10 champagne glasses or flutes. Slowly pour 2 tbsp. (30 mL) liqueur along side of glass. Allow liqueur to settle to bottom. Serves 10.

1 serving: 171 Calories; 0 g Total Fat (0 g Mono, 0 g Poly, 0 g Sat); 0 mg Cholesterol; 10 g Carbohydrate; 0 g Fibre; trace Protein; 8 mg Sodium

Pictured on page 11 and above.

Sparkling Pomegranate

The tartness of pomegranate sparkles in this effervescent cocktail. Stir to mix the layers if you want an even sweetness.

Granulated sugar	1/4 cup	60 mL
Water	1/4 cup	60 mL
Bottle of sparkling apple cider (with alcohol)	12 oz.	341 mL
Pomegranate juice	1 1/4 cups	300 mL
Bottles of sparkling dry white wine (or champagne), 25 1/2 oz., 750 mL, each, chilled	2	2

Combine sugar and water in small saucepan. Bring to a boil. Boil, uncovered, for about 1 minute until sugar is dissolved. Chill.

Combine cider, juice and sugar mixture in small pitcher. Chill.

Slowly pour about 1/4 cup (60 mL) pomegranate mixture into each of 12 champagne glasses or flutes. Slowly add 1/2 cup (125 mL) sparkling wine (see Tip, this page). Serves 12.

1 serving: 123 Calories; 0 g Total Fat (0 g Mono, 0 g Poly, 0 g Sat); 0 mg Cholesterol; 10 g Carbohydrate; 0 g Fibre; trace Protein; 9 mg Sodium

Pictured above.

Tip: *Sparkling wine will go flat quickly. If not serving all the sparkling wine at once, buy 4 smaller bottles (13 oz., 375 mL, each) and keep unopened bottles in reserve until needed.*

Rich Viennese Coffee, page 95

Tip: To bruise cardamom, pound pods with a mallet or press with the flat side of a wide knife to "bruise," or crack them open slightly.

Rich Viennese Coffee

The coffee houses of Vienna are renowned for their delightful brews as well as their flair for stimulating conversation. Bring this atmosphere home with a decadent coffee that makes the perfect after-dinner complement.

Almond liqueur	1 cup	250 mL
Hot strong prepared coffee	4 cups	1 L
Granulated sugar	1/3 cup	75 mL
Ground cinnamon	1 tsp.	5 mL
Ground cloves	1/4 tsp.	1 mL
Whipping cream	1/3 cup	75 mL
Cinnamon sticks (4 inches, 10 cm, each)	6	6

Heat liqueur in small saucepan on medium until hot, but not boiling. Cover to keep warm.

Combine next 4 ingredients in coffee pot. Stir until sugar is dissolved. Add liqueur. Stir. Pour coffee mixture into 6 mugs.

Beat cream in small bowl until soft peaks form. Spoon over coffee mixture.

Garnish with cinnamon sticks. Makes about 5 1/2 cups (1.4 L). Serves 6.

1 serving: 223 Calories; 4.8 g Total Fat (1.4 g Mono, 0.2 g Poly, 2.9 g Sat); 17 mg Cholesterol; 29 g Carbohydrate; trace Fibre; trace Protein; 11 mg Sodium

Pictured on pages 69 and 94.

Mocha Latte

This smooth, creamy latte with a perfect balance of chocolate and coffee is truly the cream of the coffee bean crop. Serve by itself or with dessert.

Milk	1 cup	250 mL
Bittersweet chocolate baking squares (1 oz., 28 g each), coarsely chopped	2	2
Milk	3 cups	750 mL
Water	4 cups	1 L
Instant coffee granules	1/2 cup	125 mL
Granulated sugar	3 tbsp.	50 mL
Whipped cream	1/2 cup	125 mL
Semi-sweet chocolate baking square (1 oz., 28 g), finely grated	1	1

Heat first amount of milk and chocolate in large saucepan on medium-low for about 5 minutes, stirring often, until chocolate is melted.

Slowly add second amount of milk, stirring constantly with whisk. Add next 3 ingredients. Heat and stir for 15 to 20 minutes until hot, but not boiling. Pour into coffee mugs.

Spoon whipped cream over top. Sprinkle with grated chocolate. Makes 8 cups.

1 serving: 244 Calories; 16.5 g Total Fat (5.3 g Mono, 0.5 g Poly, 10.0 g Sat); 35 mg Cholesterol; 21 g Carbohydrate; 2 g Fibre; 8 g Protein; 97 mg Sodium

Pictured above.

Mint Chai Latte

Chai, a south-Asian tea, can be made the traditional way for a distinctive taste experience your guests won't soon forget.

2% milk	3 cups	750 mL
Water	2 cups	500 mL
Orange pekoe tea bags	5	5
Granulated sugar	3 tbsp.	50 mL
Whole green cardamom, bruised (see Tip, this page)	6	6
Whole cloves	8	8
Cinnamon sticks (4 inches, 10 cm, each)	2	2
Dried mint	2 tsp.	10 mL
Vanilla extract	1 tsp.	5 mL
Fennel seed	1/2 tsp.	2 mL
Ground ginger	1/2 tsp.	2 mL
Ground nutmeg	1/4 tsp.	1 mL
Skim milk	1/2 cup	125 mL
Ground cinnamon, sprinkle		

Combine first 12 ingredients in large saucepan. Bring to a boil. Remove from heat. Stir. Let stand, covered, for 5 minutes. Strain through sieve. Discard solids. Cover to keep warm. Makes about 5 cups (1.25 L).

Beat skim milk with whisk or milk frother until frothy. Pour tea mixture into 4 mugs. Spoon frothed milk over top. Sprinkle with cinnamon. Serves 4.

1 serving: 146 Calories; 3.8 g Total Fat (trace Mono, 0 g Poly, 2.3 g Sat); 16 mg Cholesterol; 20 g Carbohydrate; 0 g Fibre; 7 g Protein; 110 mg Sodium

Pictured above.

Roasted Garlic Focaccia, page 97

Roasted Garlic Focaccia

An easy and quick-to-make flatbread with delicious results—and the added bonus of filling your house with that fresh bread aroma! Serve with your favourite saucy main dish. Use the quick thawing method on the package of frozen bread dough.

Garlic bulb	1	1
Olive (or cooking) oil	1 tbsp.	15 mL
Frozen white bread dough, covered, thawed in refrigerator overnight	1	1
Sesame seeds	2 tsp.	10 mL
Coarse sea salt (optional)	1/4 tsp.	1 mL

Trim 1/4 inch (6 mm) from garlic bulb to expose tops of cloves, leaving bulb intact. Wrap loosely in greased foil. Bake in 375°F (190°C) oven for about 45 minutes until tender. Let stand until cool enough to handle. Squeeze garlic bulb to remove cloves from skin. Discard skin.

Mash garlic and olive oil in small bowl.

Roll or pat out dough on lightly floured surface to 8 x 12 inch (20 x 30 cm) rectangle. Place on greased baking sheet. Cover with greased waxed paper and tea towel. Let stand in oven with light on and door closed for about 30 minutes until slightly risen. Poke indentations on surface of dough with fingers. Spread garlic mixture over dough.

Sprinkle with sesame seeds and salt. Bake in 400°F (205°C) oven for about 20 minutes until golden. Remove bread from pan and place on wire rack to cool. Cuts into 8 pieces. Serves 4.

1 serving: 330 Calories; 8.2 g Total Fat (2.8 g Mono, 0.6 g Poly, 0.6 g Sat); 0 mg Cholesterol; 51 g Carbohydrate; 4 g Fibre; 11 g Protein; 561 mg Sodium

Pictured on pages 4, 19 and 96.

Chilled Pea Dill Soup With Herbed Tortillas

This refreshing and sweet chilled soup is expertly balanced with tangy dill and buttermilk, and is accompanied with crisp herbed tortillas perfect for dunking.

Cooking oil	1 tsp.	5 mL
Chopped celery	1 cup	250 mL
Chopped onion	1 cup	250 mL
Garlic clove, minced (or 1/4 tsp., 1 mL, powder)	1	1
Salt	1/2 tsp.	2 mL
Pepper	1/4 tsp.	1 mL
Prepared vegetable broth	2 cups	500 mL
Frozen peas	2 cups	500 mL
Dried dillweed	2 tsp.	10 mL
Buttermilk	1 1/2 cups	375 mL
HERBED TORTILLAS		
Flour tortillas (9 inch, 22 cm, diameter)	2	2
Olive (or cooking) oil	1 tsp.	5 mL
Italian seasoning	1 tsp.	5 mL
Dried crushed chilies	1/2 tsp.	2 mL

Heat cooking oil in large saucepan or Dutch oven on medium. Add next 5 ingredients. Cook, uncovered, for 5 to 10 minutes, stirring often, until onion is softened.

Add broth. Bring to a boil.

Add peas and dill. Bring to a boil. Reduce heat to medium. Boil gently, uncovered, for 3 to 5 minutes until peas are tender. Carefully process with hand blender or in blender until smooth. Pour into large bowl.

Add buttermilk. Stir. Chill for 2 hours. Makes about 5 cups (1.25 L) soup.

Herbed Tortillas: Brush tortillas with olive oil.

Combine Italian seasoning and chilies in small cup. Sprinkle over tortillas. Cut into 8 wedges each. Arrange wedges on greased baking sheet. Bake in 350°F (175°C) oven for about 10 minutes until crisp and lightly browned. Makes 16 wedges. Serve with soup. Serves 4.

1 serving: 217 Calories; 5.7 g Total Fat (1.8 g Mono, 0.7 g Poly, 1.3 g Sat); 3 mg Cholesterol; 33 g Carbohydrate; 5 g Fibre; 10 g Protein; 881 mg Sodium

Pictured below.

Chilled Pea Dill Soup With Herbed Tortillas, above

Tropical Rice Salad, below

Tropical Rice Salad

This vibrantly coloured rice salad is brimming with tropical fruit and nuts, and is tossed in a refreshing pineapple dressing. It's curiously delicious!

Prepared vegetable broth	2 1/2 cups	625 mL
Turmeric	1/2 tsp.	2 mL
Long grain white rice	1 1/4 cups	300 mL
Chopped fresh (or canned) pineapple	1 cup	250 mL
Chopped fresh (or frozen, thawed) mango	3/4 cup	175 mL
Chopped celery	1/2 cup	125 mL
Chopped English cucumber (with peel)	1/2 cup	125 mL
Dried cranberries	1/3 cup	75 mL
Chopped macadamia nuts	1/4 cup	60 mL
PINEAPPLE DRESSING		
Lemon juice	1/4 cup	60 mL
Liquid honey	1/4 cup	60 mL
Pineapple juice	1/4 cup	60 mL
Garlic clove, minced	1	1
(or 1/4 tsp., 1 mL, powder)		
Salt	1/4 tsp.	1 mL
Pepper	1/8 tsp.	0.5 mL

Combine broth and turmeric in medium saucepan. Bring to a boil. Add rice. Stir. Reduce heat to medium-low. Simmer, covered, for 15 minutes, without stirring. Remove from heat. Let stand, covered, for about 5 minutes until liquid is absorbed. Transfer to plate. Spread evenly. Let stand for about 30 minutes until cool.

Combine next 6 ingredients in medium bowl. Add rice. Toss.

Pineapple Dressing: Combine all 6 ingredients in small bowl. Makes about 3/4 cup (175 mL) dressing. Pour over rice mixture. Toss gently. Makes about 6 cups (1.5 L). Serves 8.

1 serving: 233 Calories; 3.7 g Total Fat (2.6 g Mono, 0.2 g Poly, 0.6 g Sat); 0 mg Cholesterol; 47 g Carbohydrate; 2 g Fibre; 3 g Protein; 225 mg Sodium

Pictured above.

Sweet-And-Sour Beans

This unusual but tasty combination of flavours will have your guests asking for more.

Bacon slices, diced	5	5
Chopped onion	3/4 cup	175 mL
Granulated sugar	1/3 cup	75 mL
White vinegar	1/3 cup	75 mL
Fresh (or frozen) cut green beans	3 cups	750 mL

Cook bacon and onion in medium frying pan on medium for about 15 minutes, stirring often, until onion is browned and bacon is crisp. Drain and discard drippings.

Add sugar and vinegar. Heat and stir until sugar is dissolved. Remove from heat.

Pour water into medium saucepan until about 1 inch (2.5 cm) deep. Bring to a boil. Add green beans. Reduce heat to medium. Boil gently, covered, for 4 to 5 minutes until tender. Drain. Return to saucepan. Add bacon mixture. Stir. Makes about 2 3/4 cups (675 mL). Serves 4.

1 serving: 142 Calories; 3.2 g Total Fat (1.6 g Mono, 0.4 g Poly, 1.1 g Sat); 8 mg Cholesterol; 25 g Carbohydrate; 2 g Fibre; 5 g Protein; 156 mg Sodium

Polenta Triangles

Much like a spiced-up cornmeal muffin, these unusual polenta triangles are the perfect accompaniment for stews or saucy entrees.

Prepared chicken broth	4 cups	1 L
Frozen kernel corn	1/2 cup	125 mL
Garlic powder	1/2 tsp.	2 mL
Dried crushed chilies	1/4 tsp.	1 mL
Salt	1/4 tsp.	1 mL
Yellow cornmeal	1 1/2 cups	375 mL
Can of diced green chilies, drained	4 oz.	113 g
Grated Parmesan cheese	1/4 cup	60 mL
Chopped fresh parsley (or 1 1/2 tsp., 7 mL, flakes)	2 tbsp.	30 mL
Butter (or hard margarine), melted	2 tsp.	10 mL
Cooking oil	2 tsp.	10 mL

Combine first 5 ingredients in large saucepan. Bring to a boil. Reduce heat to medium.

Slowly add cornmeal, stirring constantly. Heat and stir for about 5 minutes until mixture is very thick.

Add next 3 ingredients. Stir. Spread evenly in 9 x 9 inch (22 x 22 cm) pan, lined with greased foil. Let stand at room temperature for 20 minutes. Chill for 1 hour. Invert onto cutting board. Cut in half. Cut halves crosswise into 3 rectangles each. Cut rectangles in half diagonally to make 12 triangles. Arrange triangles on greased baking sheet.

Combine melted butter and cooking oil in small cup. Brush over triangles. Broil on centre rack in oven for 10 to 15 minutes until golden and heated through. Serves 6.

1 serving: 272 Calories; 10.2 g Total Fat (3.6 g Mono, 1.1 g Poly, 5.0 g Sat); 19 mg Cholesterol; 32 g Carbohydrate; 3 g Fibre; 13 g Protein; 1497 mg Sodium

Pictured below.

Polenta Triangles, above

Mushroom Beef Consommé

This light soup with fresh mushrooms is perfect for priming the appetite for the main course.

Package of dried porcini mushrooms	3/4 oz.	22 g
Boiling water	1 cup	250 mL
Prepared beef broth	4 cups	1 L
Bay leaf	1	1
Whole clove	1	1
Butter (or hard margarine)	2 tsp.	10 mL
Sliced fresh brown (or white) mushrooms	2 cups	500 mL
Chopped fresh chives (or 1 1/2 tsp., 7 mL, dried)	2 tbsp.	30 mL
Dry sherry	1 tbsp.	15 mL
Lemon juice	1 tsp.	5 mL

Put dried mushrooms into small heatproof bowl. Add boiling water. Stir. Let stand for about 15 minutes until softened. Remove mushrooms. Strain liquid through triple layer of cheesecloth into large saucepan. Finely chop mushrooms and stems. Set aside.

Add next 3 ingredients to saucepan. Bring to a boil. Reduce heat to medium-low. Simmer, covered, for 15 minutes to blend flavours.

Melt butter in large frying pan on medium. Add brown and dried mushrooms. Cook for about 10 minutes, stirring often, until mushrooms are browned and liquid is evaporated. Add to broth mixture.

Add remaining 3 ingredients. Stir. Discard bay leaf and clove. Makes about 5 cups (1.25 L). Serves 6.

1 serving: 36 Calories; 1.6 g Total Fat (0.4 g Mono, 0.1 g Poly, 0.9 g Sat); 3 mg Cholesterol; 3 g Carbohydrate; 1 g Fibre; 2 g Protein; 784 mg Sodium

Asian Vegetable Wraps, page 101

Asian Vegetable Wraps

An inventive way of serving your dinner guests their veggies—tender-crisp in hoisin-drizzled tortillas.

Sesame (or cooking) oil	1 tsp.	5 mL
Thinly sliced red onion	1 cup	250 mL
Garlic cloves, minced (or 1/2 tsp., 2 mL, powder)	2	2
Thinly sliced red pepper	1 cup	250 mL
Thinly sliced yellow pepper	1 cup	250 mL
Can of shoestring-style bamboo shoots, drained	8 oz.	227 mL
Thinly sliced fresh shiitake mushrooms	1/2 cup	125 mL
Hoisin sauce	2 tsp.	10 mL
Soy sauce	1 tsp.	5 mL
Salt	1/2 tsp.	2 mL
Pepper	1/4 tsp.	1 mL
Fresh bean sprouts	2 cups	500 mL
Hoisin sauce	2 tbsp.	30 mL
Flour tortillas (9 inch, 22 cm, diameter)	4	4

Heat sesame oil in large frying pan on medium. Add onion and garlic. Cook for 5 to 10 minutes, stirring often, until onion is softened.

Add next 8 ingredients. Cook for 3 to 5 minutes, stirring occasionally, until peppers are tender-crisp.

Add bean sprouts. Heat and stir for 1 to 2 minutes until bean sprouts start to wilt.

Spread hoisin sauce onto tortillas. Cut tortillas in half. Spoon vegetable mixture onto tortilla halves. Fold bottom ends over filling. Fold in sides, leaving top ends open. Makes 8 wraps. Serves 4.

1 serving: 265 Calories; 6.2 g Total Fat (0.6 g Mono, 1.0 g Poly, 1.4 g Sat); trace Cholesterol; 48 g Carbohydrate; 5 g Fibre; 9 g Protein; 850 mg Sodium

Pictured on pages 39 and 100.

Chili Vegetable Ribbons

This cool and colourful medley of peppers, cucumber and carrot is marinated in a refreshingly spicy and mildly sweet mixture.

Granulated sugar	1 cup	250 mL
Water	1 cup	250 mL
White vinegar	1 cup	250 mL
Thai hot chili pepper, seeds and ribs removed, finely chopped (see Tip, below)	1	1
Salt	1/2 tsp.	2 mL
Small red pepper, thinly sliced	1	1
Small yellow pepper, thinly sliced	1	1
Large carrot	1	1
Small English cucumber (with peel)	1	1

Combine first 5 ingredients in medium saucepan. Bring to a boil. Reduce heat to medium. Boil gently, uncovered, for 5 minutes to blend flavours. Cool to room temperature.

Put red and yellow pepper into large glass bowl or jar. Using a vegetable peeler, peel long strips from carrot and cucumber. Add to peppers. Add vinegar mixture. Let stand, covered, in refrigerator for 30 minutes. Remove vegetables from vinegar mixture using slotted spoon. Arrange in large shallow bowl or plate. Pour 1/4 cup (60 mL) vinegar mixture over top. Makes about 5 cups (1.25 L). Serves 4.

1 serving: 54 Calories; 0.3 g Total Fat (trace Mono, 0.1 g Poly, trace Sat); 0 mg Cholesterol; 13 g Carbohydrate; 2 g Fibre; 1 g Protein; 88 mg Sodium

Herbed Brown Rice Pilaf

Nutty brown rice is seasoned with lemon and fresh herbs for a satisfying side.

Cooking oil	1 tbsp.	15 mL
Chopped onion	3/4 cup	175 mL
Diced carrot	1/2 cup	125 mL
Diced celery	1/2 cup	125 mL
Garlic clove, minced (or 1/4 tsp., 1 mL powder)	1	1
Dried thyme	1/4 tsp.	1 mL
Prepared chicken broth	3 cups	750 mL
Long grain brown rice	1 1/2 cups	375 mL
Finely chopped fresh basil	2 tbsp.	30 mL
Finely chopped fresh parsley	2 tbsp.	30 mL
Grated lemon zest (see Tip, page 122)	2 tsp.	10 mL
Lemon juice	2 tsp.	10 mL
Pepper	1/4 tsp.	1 mL

Heat cooking oil in large saucepan on medium. Add next 5 ingredients. Cook, uncovered, for about 5 minutes, stirring often, until vegetables are softened.

Add broth and rice. Bring to a boil. Reduce heat to medium-low. Simmer, covered, for about 50 minutes, without stirring, until liquid is almost absorbed. Remove from heat. Let stand, covered, for about 10 minutes until rice is tender and liquid is absorbed. Fluff with fork.

Add remaining 5 ingredients. Toss. Makes about 5 cups (1.25 L). Serves 6.

1 serving: 219 Calories; 4.3 g Total Fat (2.1 g Mono, 1.4 g Poly, 0.6 g Sat); 0 mg Cholesterol; 40 g Carbohydrate; 3 g Fibre; 5 g Protein; 762 mg Sodium

Tip: Hot peppers contain capsaicin in the seeds and ribs. Removing the seeds and ribs will reduce the heat. Wear rubber gloves when handling hot peppers and avoid touching your eyes. Wash your hands well afterwards.

Curried Wild Rice Pilaf

This mixture of wild rice, fresh vegetables and dried cranberry has a mild curry flavour that goes well with pork, chicken and fish.

Water	3 cups	750 mL
Salt	1/2 tsp.	2 mL
Wild rice	1 cup	250 mL
Cooking oil	1 tsp.	5 mL
Chopped fresh white mushrooms	3 cups	750 mL
Chopped red onion	1 cup	250 mL
Garlic cloves, minced (or 1/2 tsp., 2 mL, powder)	2	2
Diced red pepper	1 cup	250 mL
Diced yellow pepper	1 cup	250 mL
Dried cranberries	1 cup	250 mL
Apple juice	1/3 cup	75 mL
Curry powder	1 tsp.	5 mL
Ground cumin	1/4 tsp.	1 mL
Salt	1/2 tsp.	2 mL
Pepper	1/4 tsp.	1 mL

Combine water and salt in medium saucepan. Bring to a boil. Add rice. Stir. Reduce heat to medium-low. Simmer, covered, for about 1 hour, without stirring, until rice is tender. Drain any remaining liquid.

Heat cooking oil in large saucepan or Dutch oven on medium. Add next 3 ingredients. Cook, uncovered, for 5 to 10 minutes, stirring often, until onion is softened.

Add next 8 ingredients. Stir. Cook for 5 to 8 minutes, stirring occasionally, until vegetables are tender-crisp. Add rice. Cook and stir until heated through. Makes about 7 1/2 cups (1.9 L). Serves 8.

1 serving: 152 Calories; 1.0 g Total Fat (0.4 g Mono, 0.2 g Poly, 0.1 g Sat); 0 mg Cholesterol; 34 g Carbohydrate; 2 g Fibre; 4 g Protein; 223 mg Sodium

Pictured on pages 34, 35 and at left.

Curried Wild Rice Pilaf, right

Creamy Garlic Mashed Potatoes, below

Eggplant Zucchini Bake

This ratatouille-like vegetable casserole is packed with plenty of family-friendly Italian flavours.

Peeled eggplant, cut into 1 inch (2.5 cm) cubes	2 lbs.	900 g
Salt	2 tsp.	10 mL
All-purpose flour	1/4 cup	60 mL
Pepper	1/2 tsp.	2 mL
Zucchini (with peel), cut into 1 inch (2.5 cm) cubes	2 lbs.	900 g
Olive oil	1 tbsp.	15 mL
Olive oil	1 tbsp.	15 mL
Olive oil	1 tbsp.	15 mL
Chopped onion	1 cup	250 mL
Garlic cloves, minced (or 1/2 tsp., 2 mL, powder)	2	2
Can of diced tomatoes, drained	19 oz.	540 mL
Dried oregano	1 tsp.	5 mL
Grated mozzarella cheese	2 cups	500 mL
Chopped fresh basil (or 1 tbsp., 15 mL, dried)	1/4 cup	60 mL
Grated Parmesan cheese	2 tbsp.	30 mL

Put eggplant and salt into large bowl. Toss. Transfer to paper towel-lined baking sheets. Let stand for 30 minutes. Rinse. Pat dry.

Combine flour and pepper in shallow bowl. Add zucchini and eggplant. Toss until coated.

Brush large baking sheet with sides with first amount of olive oil. Arrange eggplant and zucchini in single layer. Drizzle with second amount of olive oil. Broil on top rack in oven for 8 to 10 minutes until browned. Transfer to 3 quart (3 L) baking dish.

Heat third amount of olive oil in large frying pan on medium. Add onion and garlic. Cook for 5 to 8 minutes, stirring often, until softened.

Add tomatoes and oregano. Heat and stir for 1 minute. Add to eggplant mixture. Stir.

Sprinkle remaining 3 ingredients over top. Bake, uncovered, in 350°F (175°C) oven for about 30 minutes until cheese is melted and golden. Makes about 8 cups (2 L). Serves 6.

1 serving: 289 Calories; 16.5 g Total Fat (7.8 g Mono, 1.1 g Poly, 6.6 g Sat); 32 mg Cholesterol; 25 g Carbohydrate; 8 g Fibre; 13 g Protein; 512 mg Sodium

Creamy Garlic Mashed Potatoes

These smooth and rich-tasting mashed potatoes are lightly infused with garlic for an elegant blending of flavours.

Peeled potatoes, cut up	5 lbs.	2.3 kg
Butter	1/3 cup	75 mL
Garlic cloves, minced (or 2 tsp., 10 mL, powder)	8	8
Milk	2/3 cup	150 mL
Sour cream	1 cup	250 mL
Dijon mustard	1 tbsp.	15 mL
Salt	1 tsp.	5 mL
Pepper	1/2 tsp.	2 mL

Pour water into Dutch oven until about 1 inch (2.5 cm) deep. Add potato. Cover. Bring to a boil. Reduce heat to medium. Boil gently, covered, for 12 to 15 minutes until tender. Drain. Mash. Cover to keep warm.

Melt butter in small frying pan on medium. Add garlic. Heat and stir for about 1 minute until fragrant. Add milk. Bring to a boil. Add to potato. Mash well.

Add remaining 4 ingredients. Stir. Makes about 10 cups (2.5 L). Serves 10.

1 serving: 303 Calories; 10.6 g Total Fat (2.8 g Mono, 0.5 g Poly, 6.6 g Sat); 27 mg Cholesterol; 48 g Carbohydrate; 4 g Fibre; 5 g Protein; 328 mg Sodium

Pictured on front cover and on pages 10, 11 and above.

Nutty Mushroom Wild Rice, page 105

Nutty Mushroom Wild Rice

The lovely contrasting textures of chewy wild rice and crunchy nuts make for a flavourful side dish. Excellent with fish or chicken.

Prepared chicken broth	2 1/4 cups	550 mL
Wild rice	3/4 cup	175 mL
Butter (or hard margarine)	1 tbsp.	15 mL
Sliced fresh white mushrooms	2 cups	500 mL
Finely chopped onion	1/3 cup	75 mL
Pine nuts, toasted (see Tip, page 79)	2 tbsp.	30 mL
Slivered almonds, toasted (see Tip, page 79)	2 tbsp.	30 mL
Pepper	1/4 tsp.	1 mL

Measure broth into medium saucepan. Bring to a boil. Add rice. Stir. Reduce heat to medium-low. Simmer, covered, for about 60 minutes, without stirring, until rice is tender. Drain any remaining liquid. Transfer to medium bowl. Cover to keep warm.

Melt butter in medium frying pan on medium. Add mushrooms and onion. Cook for 10 to 15 minutes, stirring often, until mushrooms are browned. Add to rice.

Add remaining 3 ingredients. Toss. Makes about 3 cups (750 mL). Serves 4.

1 serving: 225 Calories; 8.7 g Total Fat (3.4 g Mono, 2.2 g Poly, 2.6 g Sat); 8 mg Cholesterol; 30 g Carbohydrate; 4 g Fibre; 8 g Protein; 862 mg Sodium

Pictured on pages 40, 41 and 104.

Seeded Multigrain Quickbread

There's nothing more welcoming for your guests than the aroma of fresh bread baking in the oven. This simple, nutty loaf makes a great accompaniment to salads, soups and stews.

All-purpose flour	1 cup	250 mL
Quick-cooking rolled oats	1 cup	250 mL
Whole-wheat flour	1 cup	250 mL
Ground flaxseed	2 tbsp.	30 mL
Sesame seeds	2 tbsp.	30 mL
Sunflower seeds	2 tbsp.	30 mL
Baking powder	1 1/2 tsp.	7 mL
Baking soda	1 tsp.	5 mL
Salt	1 tsp.	5 mL
Buttermilk (or soured milk, see Tip, below)	1 3/4 cups	425 mL
Cooking oil	1/3 cup	75 mL
Poppy seeds	1 tsp.	5 mL

Measure first 9 ingredients in large bowl. Stir. Make a well in centre.

Add buttermilk and cooking oil to well. Stir until just moistened. Spread in greased 9 x 5 x 3 inch (22 x 12.5 x 7.5 cm) loaf pan.

Sprinkle poppy seeds over top. Bake in 375°F (190°C) oven for about 40 minutes until wooden pick inserted in centre comes out clean. Let stand in pan for 10 minutes. Remove loaf from pan and place on wire rack to cool. Cuts into 16 slices.

1 slice: 142 Calories; 6.7 g Total Fat (3.0 g Mono, 1.7 g Poly, 0.6 g Sat); 1 mg Cholesterol; 17 g Carbohydrate; 2 g Fibre; 4 g Protein; 279 mg Sodium

Strawberry Cucumber Soup, below

Strawberry Cucumber Soup

There's something so refined about a lovely chilled soup. Refreshing and mildly sweetened with cinnamon and ginger. Garnish with thin slices of cucumber or strawberries.

Coarsely chopped, peeled English cucumber, seeds removed	3 cups	750 mL
Frozen whole strawberries, partially thawed	3 cups	750 mL
White grape juice	1 cup	250 mL
Granulated sugar	1/4 cup	60 mL
Ground ginger	1 tsp.	5 mL
Ground cinnamon	1/4 tsp.	1 mL
Salt	1/4 tsp.	1 mL
Pepper	1/4 tsp.	1 mL
Half-and-half cream	1/2 cup	125 mL

Put cucumber into blender or food processor. Process until smooth.

Add next 7 ingredients. Process until almost smooth. Transfer to medium bowl.

Add cream. Stir. Chill. Makes about 5 1/2 cups (1.4 L). Serves 12.

1 serving: 58 Calories; 1.4 g Total Fat (0.4 g Mono, 0.1 g Poly, 0.8 g Sat); 4 mg Cholesterol; 11 g Carbohydrate; 1 g Fibre; 1 g Protein; 55 mg Sodium

Pictured on page 65 and above.

Tip: *To make soured milk, measure 1 tbsp. (15 mL) white vinegar or lemon juice into a 1 cup (250 mL) liquid measure. Add enough milk to make 1 cup (250 mL). Stir. Let stand for 1 minute.*

Slow Cooker Scallop

Traditional scalloped potatoes are always welcome at a hearty feast. And because these are made in your slow cooker, your oven will be free for any other dish your heart desires.

Butter (or hard margarine)	1/4 cup	60 mL
All-purpose flour	1/4 cup	60 mL
Milk	3 cups	750 mL
Parsley flakes	1 tbsp.	15 mL
Dried rosemary, crushed	1 tsp.	5 mL
Garlic powder	1/2 tsp.	2 mL
Salt	1 tsp.	5 mL
Pepper	1/2 tsp.	2 mL
Peeled potatoes, thinly sliced	5 lbs.	2.3 kg
Thinly sliced onion	2 cups	500 mL
Grated Parmesan cheese	1/4 cup	60 mL
Paprika	1/4 tsp.	1 mL

Melt butter in medium saucepan on medium. Add flour. Heat and stir for 1 minute. Slowly add 1 cup (250 mL) milk, stirring constantly until boiling and thickened. Add remaining milk. Cook and stir until heated through.

Add next 5 ingredients. Stir.

Put half of potato and onion into greased 5 quart (5 L) slow cooker. Pour half of sauce over top. Stir. Add remaining potato and onion. Pour remaining sauce over top. Stir. Cook, covered, on Low for 8 hours or on High for 4 hours.

Sprinkle with cheese and paprika. Let stand, covered, for 5 minutes. Makes about 11 cups (2.75 L). Serves 12.

1 serving: 252 Calories; 5.3 g Total Fat (1.4 g Mono, 0.3 g Poly, 3.2 g Sat); 15 mg Cholesterol; 46 g Carbohydrate; 4 g Fibre; 7 g Protein; 745 mg Sodium

Pictured on page 63 and at left.

Slow Cooker Scallop, right

Napa Apple Salad

This fresh, crisp, light salad with a sweet and tangy dressing makes a marvellous accompaniment to any roast.

Shredded suey choy (Chinese cabbage), lightly packed	6 cups	1.5 L
Frozen peas, thawed	2 cups	500 mL
Frozen kernel corn, thawed	1 cup	250 mL
Lemon juice	1 tsp.	5 mL
Diced unpeeled apple	2 cups	500 mL
SWEET AND TANGY DRESSING		
Apple juice	1/3 cup	75 mL
Cooking oil	1/3 cup	75 mL
Apple cider vinegar	3 tbsp.	50 mL
Maple (or maple-flavoured) syrup	2 tbsp.	30 mL
Dijon mustard (with whole seeds)	2 tsp.	10 mL
Salt	1/2 tsp.	2 mL
Pepper	1/4 tsp.	1 mL

Put first 3 ingredients into extra-large bowl. Toss.

Sprinkle lemon juice over apple in small bowl. Toss until coated. Add to cabbage mixture.

Sweet And Tangy Dressing: Combine all 7 ingredients in small bowl. Makes about 1 cup (250 mL) dressing. Drizzle over cabbage mixture. Toss until coated. Makes about 8 cups (2 L). Serves 12.

1 serving: 111 Calories; 6.4 g Total Fat (3.6 g Mono, 1.9 g Poly, 0.5 g Sat); 0 mg Cholesterol; 13 g Carbohydrate; 2 g Fibre; 2 g Protein; 166 mg Sodium

Pictured on page 63 and below.

Napa Apple Salad, above

Glazed Sesame Ginger Green Beans

Your guests will eat their vegetables and ask for more with these green beans coated in a delicious sauce of hoisin, garlic and sesame oil.

Hoisin sauce	3 tbsp.	50 mL
Rice wine (or dry sherry)	1 tbsp.	15 mL
Sesame oil (for flavour)	2 tsp.	10 mL
Boiling water	4 cups	1 L
Salt	1 tsp.	5 mL
Fresh (or frozen) whole green beans	1 lb.	454 g
Cooking oil	1 tbsp.	15 mL
Finely grated gingerroot	1 tbsp.	15 mL
Garlic cloves, minced (or 2 tsp., 10 mL powder)	2	2
Sesame seeds, toasted (see Tip, page 79)	2 tsp.	10 mL

Stir first 3 ingredients in small cup until smooth. Set aside.

Combine boiling water and salt in large saucepan. Bring to a boil. Add green beans. Boil gently, uncovered, for 2 minutes. Drain. Rinse under very cold water until cool. Drain well.

Heat cooking oil in large frying pan or wok on medium. Add next 3 ingredients. Stir-fry for 1 minute. Add hoisin sauce mixture. Heat and stir until combined. Add green beans. Stir-fry for about 2 minutes until green beans are glazed and heated through. Makes about 4 cups (1 L). Serves 6.

1 serving: 82 Calories; 4.7 g Total Fat (2.2 g Mono, 1.7 g Poly, 0.5 g Sat); trace Cholesterol; 9 g Carbohydrate; 2 g Fibre; 2 g Protein; 129 mg Sodium

Tip: To julienne, cut into very thin strips that resemble matchsticks.

Braised Fennel Medley, page 109

Braised Fennel Medley

Mild, liquorice-flavoured fennel is wonderfully complemented by sweet red peppers and carrots. This colourful side dish goes well with chicken, turkey or seafood.

Medium fennel bulbs (white part only)	2	2
Cooking oil	2 tsp.	10 mL
Cooking oil	1 tsp.	5 mL
Julienned carrot (see Tip, page 107)	1 cup	250 mL
Sliced onion	1 cup	250 mL
Thinly sliced celery	1 cup	250 mL
Garlic cloves, minced, (or 1/2 tsp., 2 mL powder)	2	2
Dried thyme	1/4 tsp.	1 mL
Salt	1/2 tsp.	2 mL
Pepper	1/4 tsp.	1 mL
Prepared vegetable broth	1 cup	250 mL
Dry (or alcohol-free) white wine	1/2 cup	125 mL
Thinly sliced red pepper	1 cup	250 mL
Grated lemon zest	1 tbsp.	15 mL

Cut fennel bulbs in half lengthwise. Cut halves lengthwise into 4 wedges each. Heat cooking oil in large frying pan on medium-high. Arrange fennel in single layer in pan. Cook for about 2 minutes per side until browned. Transfer to plate. Set aside. Reduce heat to medium.

Add second amount of cooking oil to same frying pan. Add next 7 ingredients. Cook for about 5 minutes, stirring often, until onion is softened.

Add broth, wine and fennel. Heat and stir, scraping any brown bits from bottom of pan, until boiling. Cook, covered, for about 10 minutes until fennel is tender.

Add red pepper. Stir. Simmer, uncovered, for about 5 minutes until red pepper is tender-crisp and liquid is almost evaporated.

Add lemon zest. Stir. Makes 5 cups (1.25 L). Serves 10.

1 serving: 57 Calories; 1.6 g Total Fat (0.8 g Mono, 0.5 g Poly, 0.1 g Sat); 0 mg Cholesterol; 8 g Carbohydrate; 3 g Fibre; 1 g Protein; 207 mg Sodium

Pictured on page 108.

Raspberry Greens, below

Raspberry Greens

This attractive plated salad includes a refreshing raspberry dressing. Topped with avocado and fresh raspberries, it's fascinatingly delicious. Try with strawberries, blueberries or dried cranberries for a customized variation.

RASPBERRY DRESSING

Olive oil	1/4 cup	60 mL
Raspberry vinegar	2 tbsp.	30 mL
Sweet chili sauce	1 tbsp.	15 mL
Liquid honey	1 tsp.	5 mL
Garlic clove, minced (or 1/4 tsp., 1 mL powder)	1	1
Dijon mustard	1/2 tsp.	2 mL
Salt	1/2 tsp.	2 mL

SALAD

Spring mix lettuce, lightly packed	6 cups	1.5 L
Large ripe avocado, sliced	1	1
Fresh raspberries	1 cup	250 mL
Chopped green onion	2 tbsp.	30 mL

Raspberry Dressing: Whisk all 7 ingredients in small bowl. Makes about 1/2 cup (125 mL) dressing.

Salad: Put lettuce into large bowl. Drizzle with dressing. Toss. Arrange on 4 salad plates. Arrange avocado and raspberries over top. Sprinkle with green onion. Serves 4.

1 serving: 248 Calories; 21.1 g Total Fat (14.9 g Mono, 2.2 g Poly, 2.9 g Sat); 0 mg Cholesterol; 15 g Carbohydrate; 6 g Fibre; 2 g Protein; 494 mg Sodium

Pictured on pages 40, 41 and above.

Cornbread Deluxe

Although a favourite staple in the South, cornbread is a delicious, but often forgotten, side. Give your guests a treat.

All-purpose flour	2 cups	500 mL
Yellow cornmeal	2 cups	500 mL
Grated sharp Cheddar cheese	1 cup	250 mL
Granulated sugar	1/4 cup	60 mL
Chopped fresh chives (or 1 1/2 tsp., 7 mL, dried)	2 tbsp.	30 mL
Baking powder	4 tsp.	20 mL
Baking soda	1 1/2 tsp.	7 mL
Chili powder	1 tsp.	5 mL
Grated lime zest	1 tsp.	5 mL
Salt	1 tsp.	5 mL
Large eggs	4	4
Buttermilk (or soured milk, see Tip, page 105)	2 cups	500 mL
Butter (or hard margarine), melted	2/3 cup	150 mL

Measure first 10 ingredients into large bowl. Stir. Make a well in centre.

Whisk remaining 3 ingredients in medium bowl. Add to well. Stir until just moistened. Spread in greased 9 x 13 inch (22 x 33 cm) baking dish. Bake in 400°F (205°C) oven for about 25 minutes until wooden pick inserted in centre comes out clean. Cuts into 12 pieces.

1 piece: 337 Calories; 15.6 g Total Fat (4.4 g Mono, 0.9 g Poly, 9.2 g Sat); 100 mg Cholesterol; 39 g Carbohydrate; 2 g Fibre; 10 g Protein; 636 mg Sodium

Citrus Pecan Salad, right

Citrus Pecan Salad

There's lots of colour and flavour in this crowd-pleasing salad. For an extra-special presentation, use dark mixed greens for a greater colour contrast. You may want to make extra pecans because your guests will be clamouring for more!

Brown sugar, packed	1/4 cup	60 mL
Butter	1 tbsp.	15 mL
Pecan halves	1 cup	250 mL
Mixed salad greens, lightly packed	10 cups	2.5 L
Orange segments (see Tip, page 113)	1 cup	250 mL
Pomegranate seeds	1 cup	250 mL

CITRUS DRESSING

Olive (or cooking) oil	1/4 cup	60 mL
Lemon juice	2 tbsp.	30 mL
Orange juice	2 tbsp.	30 mL
Grated orange zest (see Tip, page 122)	1 tbsp.	15 mL
Liquid honey	2 tsp.	10 mL
Salt, sprinkle		
Pepper, sprinkle		

Heat brown sugar and butter in small saucepan on medium, stirring often, until sugar is dissolved. Add pecans. Stir until coated. Spread evenly on greased baking sheet with sides. Bake in 350°F (175°C) oven for about 8 minutes, stirring once, until caramelized. Let stand, stirring occasionally, until cooled.

Put next 3 ingredients into large bowl. Toss.

Citrus Dressing: Combine all 7 ingredients in jar with tight-fitting lid. Shake well. Makes about 2/3 cup (150 mL) dressing. Drizzle over lettuce mixture. Add pecans. Toss. Makes about 11 cups (2.75 L). Serves 10.

1 serving: 201 Calories; 15.1 g Total Fat (9.1 g Mono, 3.0 g Poly, 2.2 g Sat); 3 mg Cholesterol; 17 g Carbohydrate; 2 g Fibre; 2 g Protein; 18 mg Sodium

Pictured on front cover, page 10 and at left.

Spinach Risotto

Fans of risotto are sure to love this creamy spinach and dill mixture that's a perfect side to any entree. Use fresh Parmesan cheese for best results.

Prepared vegetable broth	6 cups	1.5 L
Olive (or cooking) oil	1 tbsp.	15 mL
Finely chopped onion	1/2 cup	125 mL
Arborio rice	1 1/2 cups	375 mL
Box of frozen chopped spinach, thawed and squeezed dry	10 oz.	300 g
Grated fresh Parmesan cheese	1/2 cup	125 mL
Chopped fresh dill	2 tbsp.	30 mL

Measure broth into medium saucepan. Bring to a boil. Reduce heat to low. Cover to keep hot.

Heat olive oil in large saucepan or Dutch oven on medium. Add onion. Cook, uncovered, for about 5 minutes, stirring often, until softened.

Add rice. Stir until coated. Add 1/2 cup (125 mL) hot broth, stirring constantly, until broth is almost absorbed. Repeat with remaining broth, 1/2 cup (125 mL) at a time, until broth is absorbed and rice is tender.

Add remaining 3 ingredients. Stir until heated through. Makes about 6 cups (1.5 L). Serves 10.

1 serving: *177 Calories; 3.6 g Total Fat (1.4 g Mono, 0.2 g Poly, 1.2 g Sat); 4 mg Cholesterol; 33 g Carbohydrate; 2 g Fibre; 6 g Protein; 390 mg Sodium*

Pictured below.

Note: Most standard ladles have 1/2 cup (125 mL) capacity.

Mushroom Barley Pilaf

Packed with porcinis, this flavourful pilaf goes excellently with roasted or grilled meats.

Package of dried porcini mushrooms	3/4 oz.	22 g
Boiling water	1 cup	250 mL
Cooking oil	1 tbsp.	15 mL
Chopped fresh brown (or white) mushrooms	2 cups	500 mL
Chopped onion	1 cup	250 mL
Butter (or hard margarine)	1 tbsp.	15 mL
Pearl barley	1 1/2 cups	375 mL
Prepared chicken broth	2 1/2 cups	625 mL
Lemon juice (or white wine)	1 tbsp.	15 mL
Salt	1/4 tsp.	1 mL
Pepper	1/4 tsp.	1 mL

Put dried mushrooms into small heatproof bowl. Add boiling water. Stir. Let stand for about 15 minutes until softened. Remove mushrooms. Strain liquid through triple layer of cheesecloth into small bowl. Set aside. Chop mushrooms and stems.

Heat cooking oil in large saucepan on medium. Add brown mushrooms, onion and dried chopped mushrooms and stems. Cook, uncovered, for 5 to 10 minutes, stirring often, until onion is softened and mushrooms are browned.

Add butter and barley. Heat and stir for about 2 minutes until barley is coated. Add remaining 4 ingredients and reserved mushroom liquid. Bring to a boil. Reduce heat to medium-low. Simmer, covered, for about 40 minutes until barley is tender and liquid is absorbed. Makes about 6 cups (1.5 L). Serves 8.

1 serving: *189 Calories; 4.1 g Total Fat (1.6 g Mono, 0.9 g Poly, 1.2 g Sat); 3.8 mg Cholesterol; 34 g Carbohydrate; 4 g Fibre; 5 g Protein; 553 mg Sodium*

Spinach Risotto, above

Bittersweet Apple Salad, page 113

Bittersweet Apple Salad

This unusual bittersweet taste experience is achieved by pairing radicchio with a sweet apple vinaigrette. Great for the guests who like to experiment with unique flavours.

APPLE VINAIGRETTE

Apple jelly	1/4 cup	60 mL
Apple cider vinegar	3 tbsp.	50 mL
Olive (or cooking) oil	2 tbsp.	30 mL
Dry mustard	1/2 tsp.	2 mL
Salt	1/4 tsp.	1 mL
Pepper, sprinkle		

SALAD

Cut or torn butter lettuce, lightly packed	6 cups	1.5 L
Cut or torn radicchio, lightly packed	4 cups	1 L
Diced unpeeled cooking apple (such as McIntosh)	1 cup	250 mL
Sliced yellow (or red) pepper	1/2 cup	125 mL

Apple Vinaigrette: Put jelly into small microwave-safe bowl. Microwave, uncovered, on medium (50%) for about 1 minute until melted.

Put next 5 ingredients into blender. Add jelly. Process until smooth. Makes about 2/3 cup (150 mL) vinaigrette.

Salad: Put all 4 ingredients into large bowl. Toss. Drizzle with dressing. Toss. Makes about 12 cups (3 L). Serves 6.

1 serving: 103 Calories; 4.8 g Total Fat (3.4 g Mono, 0.5 g Poly, 0.7 g Sat); 0 mg Cholesterol; 15 g Carbohydrate; 2 g Fibre; 1 g Protein; 121 mg Sodium

Pictured on page 112.

Pictured on page 112.

Tip: *To segment an orange, trim a small slice of peel from both ends so the flesh is exposed. Place the orange, bottom cut-side down, on a cutting board. Remove the peel with a sharp knife, cutting down and around the flesh, leaving as little pith as possible. Over a small bowl, cut on either side of the membranes to release the segments.*

Orange Jicama Salad

This beautiful layered jicama (pronounced HEE-kah-mah) salad has contrasting crisp and tender textures and a sweet and spicy dressing. It makes a flavourful feast for the eyes and the palate.

POMEGRANATE DRESSING

Cooking oil	1 tsp.	5 mL
Finely chopped red onion	1/4 cup	60 mL
Finely chopped jalapeño pepper (see Tip, page 101)	1 tbsp.	15 mL
Garlic clove, minced (or 1/4 tsp., 1 mL, powder)	1	1
Pomegranate juice	1/4 cup	60 mL
Olive (or cooking) oil	2 tbsp.	30 mL
Finely chopped fresh cilantro	1 tbsp.	15 mL
Maple (or maple-flavoured) syrup	1 tbsp.	15 mL
Grated lime zest	1 tsp.	5 mL
Salt	1/2 tsp.	2 mL

SALAD

Mixed salad greens, lightly packed	4 cups	1 L
Shredded peeled jicama	2 cups	500 mL
Thinly sliced red onion	1/4 cup	60 mL
Medium oranges, segmented (see Tip, this page)	2	2
Pine nuts, toasted (see Tip, page 79)	2 tbsp.	30 mL

Pomegranate Dressing: Heat cooking oil in small frying pan on medium. Add next 3 ingredients. Cook for about 5 minutes, stirring often, until onion is golden. Transfer to small bowl.

Add next 6 ingredients. Process with hand blender or in blender until combined. Makes about 1/2 cup (125 mL) dressing.

Salad: Layer all 5 ingredients, in order given, on 4 plates. Drizzle with Pomegranate Dressing. Serves 4.

1 serving: 200 Calories; 10.5 g Total Fat (6.6 g Mono, 2.0 g Poly, 1.4 g Sat); 0 mg Cholesterol; 27 g Carbohydrate; 8 g Fibre; 3 g Protein; 305 mg Sodium

Pictured on page 23 and below.

Pictured on page 23 and below.

Orange Jicama Salad, above

Walnut And Pear Salad

Delightful to the eye and delicious to eat! Candied walnuts and sweet pears are perfectly matched with mixed greens and a drizzle of honey-Dijon dressing.

Butter (or hard margarine)	2 tsp.	10 mL
Liquid honey	2 tbsp.	30 mL
Ground allspice	1/2 tsp.	2 mL
Walnut pieces	1 1/2 cups	375 mL

HONEY DIJON DRESSING

Olive oil	1/3 cup	75 mL
Red wine vinegar	1/4 cup	60 mL
Liquid honey	3 tbsp.	50 mL
Dijon mustard	2 tsp.	10 mL
Ground ginger	1 tsp.	5 mL
Salt	1/4 tsp.	1 mL
Pepper	1/4 tsp.	1 mL

SALAD

Spring mix lettuce, lightly packed	6 cups	1.5 L
Large unpeeled pears, thinly sliced	2	2
Grated smoked Gouda cheese	1/2 cup	125 mL

Combine first 3 ingredients in small frying pan. Heat and stir on medium until butter is melted. Add walnuts. Heat and stir until bubbling and golden. Transfer to greased baking sheet. Let stand on wire rack for about 30 minutes, stirring occasionally, until cool.

Honey Dijon Dressing: Combine all 7 ingredients in jar with tight-fitting lid. Shake well. Makes about 2/3 cup (150 mL) dressing.

Salad: Put lettuce into large bowl. Add half of dressing. Toss. Spoon lettuce mixture onto 6 plates. Arrange pear slices over lettuce in fan shape. Sprinkle with cheese and walnuts. Drizzle with remaining dressing. Serves 6.

1 serving: 464 Calories; 36.0 g Total Fat (12.7 g Mono, 15.3 g Poly, 6.3 g Sat); 16 mg Cholesterol; 32 g Carbohydrate; 5 g Fibre; 8 g Protein; 229 mg Sodium

Pictured at left.

Walnut And Pear Salad, right

Spinach Garlic Soup

This velvety smooth soup makes a wonderful starter or side.

Cooking oil	2 tsp.	10 mL
Butter (or hard margarine)	2 tsp.	10 mL
Sliced leek (white part only)	1 1/2 cups	375 mL
Diced peeled potato	1 cup	250 mL
Garlic cloves, minced (or 3/4 tsp., 4 mL, powder)	3	3
Fresh spinach leaves, lightly packed (or box of frozen spinach, 10 oz., 300 g, thawed and squeezed dry)	10 cups	2.5 L
Ground nutmeg	1/8 tsp.	0.5 mL
Salt	1/4 tsp.	1 mL
Pepper	1/8 tsp.	0.5 mL
Prepared chicken broth	4 cups	1 L
Whipping cream	1/4 cup	60 mL

Heat cooking oil and butter in large saucepan on medium. Add next 3 ingredients. Cook, uncovered, for about 10 minutes, stirring occasionally, until leek is softened.

Add next 4 ingredients. Cook, uncovered, for 2 to 4 minutes, stirring occasionally, until spinach is wilted.

Add broth. Bring to a boil. Reduce heat to medium-low. Simmer, covered, for about 10 minutes until potato is tender. Carefully process with hand blender or in blender until smooth (see Safety Tip).

Add cream. Stir. Makes about 6 1/2 cups (1.6 L). Serves 4.

1 serving: 186 Calories; 11.0 g Total Fat (3.8 g Mono, 1.5 g Poly, 5.0 g Sat); 24 mg Cholesterol; 19 g Carbohydrate; 3 g Fibre; 5 g Protein; 1717 mg Sodium

Pictured below.

Safety Tip: Follow blender manufacturer's instructions for processing hot liquids. If in doubt, we recommend using a hand blender.

Spinach Garlic Soup, above

Spaetzle With Caramelized Onions

These uniquely shaped, tender little noodles are a delight to eat! Goes well with a saucy stew.

Butter (or hard margarine)	1/4 cup	60 mL
Chopped onion	1 1/2 cups	375 mL
All-purpose flour	2 1/4 cups	550 mL
Baking powder	1/4 tsp.	1 mL
Salt	1/2 tsp.	2 mL
Pepper	1/4 tsp.	1 mL
Large eggs	3	3
Milk	3/4 cup	175 mL
Water	1/4 cup	60 mL
Cooking oil	2 tbsp.	30 mL
Water	12 cups	3 L
Salt	1 1/2 tsp.	7 mL

Melt butter in large frying pan on medium. Add onion. Cook for about 15 minutes, stirring often, until onion is caramelized. Cover to keep warm.

Measure next 4 ingredients into medium bowl. Stir. Make a well in centre.

Beat next 4 ingredients in small bowl. Add to well. Mix to form soft batter.

Combine water and salt in Dutch oven. Bring to a boil. Place large metal colander at an angle over boiling water. Press half of batter through holes in colander. Boil, uncovered, for 1 minute, stirring occasionally. Remove noodles with sieve. Drain well. Transfer to large greased baking dish. Cover to keep warm. Repeat with remaining batter. Add onion mixture. Toss. Makes about 5 1/2 cups (1.4 L). Serves 6.

1 serving: 324 Calories; 14.9 g Total Fat (5.8 g Mono, 2.0 g Poly, 6.1 g Sat); 115 mg Cholesterol; 39 g Carbohydrate; 1 g Fibre; 9 g Protein; 307 mg Sodium

Pictured on page 16.

Grilled Balsamic Vegetables, page 117

Grilled Balsamic Vegetables

Serve these sweet, balsamic-glazed veggies on skewers for a more novel approach to dining.

BALSAMIC GLAZE

Orange juice	1/3 cup	75 mL
Balsamic vinegar	1/4 cup	60 mL
Maple (or maple-flavoured) syrup	1/4 cup	60 mL
Dijon mustard	1 tbsp.	15 mL
Salt	1/4 tsp.	1 mL
Pepper	1/4 tsp.	1 mL

SKEWERS

Red pepper pieces, about 1 inch (2.5 cm)	16	16
Yellow pepper pieces, about 1 inch (2.5 cm)	16	16
Fresh whole white mushrooms	16	16
Zucchini slices (with peel), about 1/2 inch (12 mm), cut in half	8	8
Cherry tomatoes	8	8
Bamboo skewers (8 inch, 20 cm, each), soaked in water for 10 minutes	8	8

Balsamic Glaze: Combine all 6 ingredients in small saucepan. Bring to a boil. Reduce heat to medium. Boil gently, uncovered, for about 10 minutes until slightly thickened. Makes about 1/2 cup (125 mL) glaze.

Skewers: Thread first 5 ingredients alternately onto skewers. Preheat gas barbecue to medium. Cook skewers on greased grill for 10 to 15 minutes, turning occasionally and brushing with Balsamic Glaze, until vegetables are tender. Serves 8.

1 serving: 55 Calories; 0.3 g Total Fat (trace Mono, 0.1 g Poly, 0.1 g Sat); 0 mg Cholesterol; 13 g Carbohydrate; 1 g Fibre; 2 g Protein; 105 mg Sodium

Pictured on pages 35 and 116.

Island Greens Salad

Packed with lettuce, cabbage, red onion, tomatoes and cucumber, this fantastic salad with a spicy maple dressing has to be experienced to be believed.

ISLAND DRESSING

Mayonnaise	3 tbsp.	50 mL
Maple (or maple-flavoured) syrup	1 tbsp.	15 mL
Rice vinegar	1 tbsp.	15 mL
Finely chopped fresh jalapeño pepper (see Tip, page 101)	1 tsp.	5 mL
Finely grated gingerroot (or 1/4 tsp., 1 mL, ground ginger)	1 tsp.	5 mL
Soy sauce	1 tsp.	5 mL
Grated lime zest	1/2 tsp.	2 mL
Sesame oil (for flavour)	1/2 tsp.	2 mL

SALAD

Cut or torn red leaf lettuce, lightly packed	2 cups	500 mL
Cut or torn romaine lettuce, lightly packed	2 cups	500 mL
Shredded red cabbage, lightly packed	2 cups	500 mL
Cherry tomatoes, halved	18	18
English cucumber (with peel), halved lengthwise and cut crosswise into thin slices	1 cup	250 mL
Thinly sliced red onion	1/4 cup	60 mL

Island Dressing: Process all 8 ingredients in blender until smooth. Makes about 1/3 cup (75 mL) dressing.

Salad: Put all 6 ingredients into large bowl. Drizzle with Island Dressing. Toss until coated. Makes about 8 cups (2 L). Serves 6.

1 serving: 77 Calories; 4.2 g Total Fat (2.2 g Mono, 1.5 g Poly, 0.4 g Sat); 2 mg Cholesterol; 10 g Carbohydrate; 2 g Fibre; 2 g Protein; 105 mg Sodium

Pictured below.

Island Greens Salad, above

Lemon Split Pea Soup

The traditional thick and hearty pea soup is given an update with a lively light lemon finish.

Cooking oil	2 tsp.	10 mL
Diced onion	1 cup	250 mL
Diced carrot	1 cup	250 mL
Diced celery	1 cup	250 mL
Dried oregano	1 tsp.	5 mL
Garlic clove, minced, (or 1/4 tsp., 1 mL powder)	1	1
Dried basil	1/2 tsp.	2 mL
Prepared chicken broth	6 cups	1.5 L
Yellow split peas, rinsed and drained	1 1/2 cups	375 mL
Bay leaf	1	1
Chopped fresh spinach leaves, lightly packed	1 1/2 cups	375 mL
Lemon juice	3 tbsp.	50 mL
Pepper	1/2 tsp.	2 mL

Heat cooking oil in large saucepan on medium-high. Add onion. Cook, uncovered, for about 5 minutes, stirring often, until onion is softened and starting to brown. Reduce heat to medium.

Add next 5 ingredients. Cook, uncovered, for about 5 minutes, stirring occasionally, until carrot starts to soften.

Add next 3 ingredients. Stir. Bring to a boil. Reduce heat to medium-low. Simmer, covered, for about 1 1/2 hours until peas are soft but not mushy. Discard bay leaf.

Add spinach. Heat and stir for about 1 minute until spinach is wilted. Add lemon juice and pepper. Stir. Makes about 6 cups (1.5 L). Serves 8.

1 serving: 180 Calories; 2.1 g Total Fat (1.0 g Mono, 0.7 g Poly, 0.3 g Sat); 0 mg Cholesterol; 30 g Carbohydrate; 1 g Fibre; 11 g Protein; 1141 mg Sodium

Pictured at left.

Lemon Split Pea Soup, right

Fiesta Rice, below

Fiesta Rice

This colourful Mexican-inspired rice is packed with cucumber, sweet corn and black beans. Accented with fresh lime and infused with cumin, it makes a festive side for any occasion.

Butter (or hard margarine)	2 tbsp.	30 mL
Long grain white rice	1 cup	250 mL
Finely chopped onion	1/2 cup	125 mL
Garlic cloves, minced	2	2
(or 1/2 tsp., 2 mL, powder)		
Cumin seed	1 tsp.	5 mL
Prepared chicken broth	2 1/2 cups	625 mL
Dried oregano	1/2 tsp.	2 mL
Can of black beans, rinsed and drained	19 oz.	540 mL
Frozen kernel corn, thawed	1 cup	250 mL
Diced English cucumber (with peel)	1/2 cup	125 mL
Lime juice	3 tbsp.	50 mL
Chopped fresh cilantro or parsley	1 tbsp.	15 mL
Chopped green onion	1 tbsp.	15 mL

Lime wedges, for garnish

Melt butter in large saucepan on medium. Add next 4 ingredients. Cook for 3 to 5 minutes, stirring often, until rice starts to turn golden.

Add broth and oregano. Bring to a boil. Reduce heat to medium-low. Simmer, covered, for about 20 minutes, without stirring, until liquid is almost absorbed. Fluff with fork.

Add beans and corn. Toss gently. Let stand, covered, for about 5 minutes until heated through.

Add cucumber and lime juice. Toss. Transfer to serving bowl. Sprinkle with cilantro and green onion.

Garnish with lime wedges. Makes about 7 cups (1.75 L). Serves 4.

1 serving: 373 Calories; 7.1 g Total Fat (1.9 g Mono, 0.6 g Poly, 3.9 g Sat); 15 mg Cholesterol; 70 g Carbohydrate; 8 g Fibre; 11 g Protein; 1525 mg Sodium

Pictured on page 23 and above.

Green Pea Salad

This unique lettuce-free salad gets plenty of vibrant green from celery and peas. It's combined with a delicate dill dressing for a new taste experience. Goes well with most entrees.

Frozen peas, thawed	2 cups	500 mL
Diced peeled English cucumber	1 cup	250 mL
Sliced fresh white mushrooms	1 cup	250 mL
Diced red pepper	1/2 cup	125 mL
Finely diced celery	1/2 cup	125 mL
DILL DRESSING		
Cooking oil	2 tbsp.	30 mL
Granulated sugar	2 tbsp.	30 mL
Mayonnaise	2 tbsp.	30 mL
White vinegar	2 tbsp.	30 mL
Dried dillweed	1/2 tsp.	2 mL
Seasoned salt	1/2 tsp.	2 mL

Combine first 5 ingredients in medium bowl.

Dill Dressing: Stir next 6 ingredients in small bowl until sugar is dissolved. Makes about 1/2 cup (125 mL) dressing. Pour over mushroom mixture. Toss until coated. Makes about 5 cups (1.25 L). Serves 6.

1 serving: 127 Calories; 7.2 g Total Fat (4.0 g Mono, 2.3 g Poly, 0.5 g Sat); 1 mg Cholesterol; 13 g Carbohydrate; 3 g Fibre; 3 g Protein; 211 mg Sodium

Paella Primavera, page 121

Paella Primavera

This paella (pronounced pi-AY-yuh) is the perfect alternative to plain rice. Although saffron can be a little pricey, it's worth it in this amazing side.

Saffron threads, crumbled (or turmeric)	1/4 tsp.	1 mL
Lemon juice	2 tsp.	10 mL
Bacon slices, diced	2	2
Olive oil	2 tsp.	10 mL
Chopped onion	1 cup	250 mL
Arborio rice	1 cup	250 mL
Garlic clove, minced (or 1/4 tsp., 1 mL, powder)	1	1
Dried crushed chilies	1/4 tsp.	1 mL
Prepared chicken broth	2 cups	500 mL
Sliced red pepper	1/2 cup	125 mL
Sliced yellow pepper	1/2 cup	125 mL
Dry (or alcohol-free) white wine	1/3 cup	75 mL
Paprika	1/4 tsp.	1 mL
Frozen whole green beans, halved	1/2 cup	125 mL
Frozen peas	1/4 cup	60 mL
Large pitted green olives	1/4 cup	60 mL
Pitted whole black olives	1/4 cup	60 mL
Chopped fresh basil	1 tbsp.	15 mL

Stir saffron into lemon juice in small cup. Set aside.

Cook bacon uncovered in Dutch oven on medium until crisp. Transfer to paper towel-lined plate to drain. Set aside.

Heat 1 tsp. (5 mL) drippings in same Dutch oven. Add olive oil and onion. Cook, uncovered, for 5 to 10 minutes, stirring often, until onion is softened.

Add next 3 ingredients. Heat and stir for 2 minutes.

Add next 5 ingredients, bacon and saffron mixture. Stir. Bring to a boil. Reduce heat to medium-low. Simmer, covered, for about 20 minutes, without stirring, until rice is just tender.

Add next 4 ingredients. Stir. Cook, covered, for about 5 minutes until green beans are tender. Transfer to large serving bowl.

Sprinkle with basil. Makes about 5 cups (1.25 L). Serves 6.

1 serving: 217 Calories; 6.7 g Total Fat (2.9 g Mono, 0.8 g Poly, 0.7 g Sat); 3 mg Cholesterol; 34 g Carbohydrate; 3 g Fibre; 5 g Protein; 784 mg Sodium

Pictured on page 120.

Spinach Strawberry Salad, below

Buttery Roasted Baby Potatoes

These spiced, buttery potatoes will go well with grilled or roasted meats.

Red baby potatoes, larger ones cut in half	2 lbs.	900 g
Salt	1/4 tsp.	1 mL
Butter (or hard margarine), melted	1/3 cup	75 mL
Parsley flakes	2 tsp.	10 mL
Cajun seasoning	1 1/2 tsp.	7 mL
Coarse salt	1/2 tsp.	2 mL

Place ungreased 9 x 13 inch (22 x 33 cm) baking dish in 425°F (220°C) oven. Pour water into medium saucepan until 1 inch (2.5 cm) deep. Add potatoes and salt. Cover. Bring to a boil. Reduce heat to medium. Boil gently, covered, for about 5 minutes until potatoes are starting to soften. Drain.

Drizzle butter over potatoes. Toss. Add parsley and Cajun seasoning. Toss until coated. Remove hot baking dish from oven. Add potatoes. Bake for about 30 minutes, stirring at halftime, until golden.

Sprinkle with salt. Makes about 4 cups (1 L). Serves 6.

1 serving: 214 Calories; 10.1 g Total Fat (2.6 g Mono, 0.4 g Poly, 6.4 g Sat); 27 mg Cholesterol; 27 g Carbohydrate; 2 g Fibre; 4 g Protein; 411 mg Sodium

Spinach Strawberry Salad

Give your guests a taste of summer with this fresh spinach and sweet strawberry salad dressed in a matching strawberry vinaigrette.

Fresh spinach leaves, lightly packed	8 cups	2 L
Sliced fresh strawberries	2 cups	500 mL
Diced Gouda cheese	1 cup	250 mL
STRAWBERRY DRESSING		
Olive (or cooking) oil	1/4 cup	60 mL
Strawberry jam, warmed	3 tbsp.	50 mL
Chopped fresh basil	2 tbsp.	30 mL
White wine vinegar	2 tbsp.	30 mL
Dijon mustard	1 tsp.	5 mL
Pepper	1/4 tsp.	1 mL

Arrange spinach on 8 plates. Top with strawberries and cheese.

Strawberry Dressing: Whisk all 6 ingredients in small bowl. Makes about 2/3 cup (150 mL) dressing. Drizzle over salads. Serves 8.

1 serving: 159 Calories; 11.6 g Total Fat (6.3 g Mono, 0.8 g Poly, 3.9 g Sat); 19 mg Cholesterol; 10 g Carbohydrate; 2 g Fibre; 5 g Protein; 170 mg Sodium

Pictured on page 30 and above.

Tomato Salad With Orange Basil Dressing

This colourful combination of contrasting textures and tastes is accented with a slightly sweet and tangy dressing.

Halved cherry tomatoes	2 cups	500 mL
Chopped English cucumber (with peel)	1 cup	250 mL
Frozen (or canned) kernel corn, thawed	1 cup	250 mL

ORANGE BASIL DRESSING		
Frozen concentrated orange juice	2 tbsp.	30 mL
Chopped fresh basil (or 3/4 tsp., 4 mL, dried)	1 tbsp.	15 mL
Olive oil	1 tbsp.	15 mL
Apple cider vinegar	2 tsp.	10 mL
Dijon mustard	1 tsp.	5 mL
Grated orange zest	1/2 tsp.	2 mL
Liquid honey	1/2 tsp.	2 mL
Salt	1/4 tsp.	1 mL
Pepper	1/8 tsp.	0.5 mL

Combine first 3 ingredients in medium bowl.

Orange Basil Dressing: Combine all 9 ingredients in small jar with tight-fitting lid. Shake well. Makes about 1/4 cup (60 mL) dressing. Drizzle over tomato mixture. Toss. Let stand for 30 minutes, stirring occasionally. Makes about 4 cups (1 L). Serves 4.

1 serving: 95 Calories; 3.8 g Total Fat (2.5 g Mono, 0.4 g Poly, 0.5 g Sat); 0 mg Cholesterol; 15 g Carbohydrate; 2 g Fibre; 2 g Protein; 169 mg Sodium

Pictured at left.

Tip: *When a recipe calls for grated lemon zest and juice, it's easier to grate the lemon first, then juice it. Be careful not to grate down to the pith (white part of the peel), which is bitter and best avoided.*

Tomato Salad With Orange Basil Dressing, right

Tomato Basil Salad, below

Lemon Herb Linguine

This simple herbed linguine delights without taking anything away from your star attraction. Serve with additional Parmesan cheese and freshly ground pepper. Perfect with fish or chicken and Caesar salad.

Water	12 cups	3 L
Salt	1 1/2 tsp.	7 mL
Linguine	12 oz.	340 g
Olive (or cooking) oil	3 tbsp.	50 mL
Chopped onion	1 1/2 cups	375 mL
Garlic cloves, minced	2	2
(or 1/2 tsp., 2 mL, powder)		
Fennel seed	1/4 tsp.	1 mL
Lemon juice	2 tbsp.	30 mL
Balsamic vinegar	1 tbsp.	15 mL
Grated lemon zest (see Tip, page 122)	2 tsp.	10 mL
Chopped fresh basil	1 tbsp.	15 mL
(or 3/4 tsp., 4 mL, dried), see Note		
Chopped fresh parsley	1 tbsp.	15 mL
(or 3/4 tsp., 4 mL, flakes)		
Chopped fresh thyme	2 tsp.	10 mL
(or 1/2 tsp., 2 mL, dried), see Note		
Chopped fresh oregano	1 tsp.	5 mL
(or 1/4 tsp., 1 mL, dried), see Note		
Grated Parmesan cheese	**1/4 cup**	**60 mL**

Combine water and salt in Dutch oven. Bring to a boil. Add pasta. Boil, uncovered, for 8 to 10 minutes, stirring occasionally, until tender but firm. Drain. Return to same pot. Cover to keep warm.

Heat olive oil in medium frying pan on medium. Add next 3 ingredients. Cook for 5 to 10 minutes, stirring often, until onion is softened.

Add next 3 ingredients. Heat and stir for 1 minute. Add to pasta.

Add next 4 ingredients. Toss.

Sprinkle with cheese. Makes about 5 1/2 cups (1.4 L). Serves 6.

1 serving: 308 Calories; 8.9 g Total Fat (5.4 g Mono, 0.6 g Poly, 2.0 g Sat); 3 mg Cholesterol; 48 g Carbohydrate; 3 g Fibre; 10 g Protein; 83 mg Sodium

Note: If you prefer to use dried herbs, add them with the fennel seed when cooking onions.

Tomato Basil Salad

The fresh, natural flavours of tomato and basil are at their best when accented with a creamy pepper dressing. Use ripe tomatoes for best results.

Butter lettuce leaves	16	16
Tomato slices,	24	24
1/4 inch (6 mm)		
thick		
PEPPER CREAM DRESSING		
Buttermilk	3 tbsp.	50 mL
Sour cream	3 tbsp.	50 mL
Dijon mustard	1 tbsp.	15 mL
White wine vinegar	1 tbsp.	15 mL
Coarsely ground	1/2 tsp.	2 mL
pepper		
Chopped fresh basil	1/4 cup	60 mL

Arrange lettuce leaves on 4 plates. Arrange 6 tomato slices in overlapping circle over lettuce on each plate.

Pepper Cream Dressing: Combine first 5 ingredients in small bowl. Makes about 1/2 cup (125 mL) dressing. Drizzle over salads.

Sprinkle with basil. Serves 4.

1 serving: 56 Calories; 2.4 g Total Fat (0.7 g Mono, 0.3 g Poly, 1.3 g Sat); 5 mg Cholesterol; 7 g Carbohydrate; 2 g Fibre; 3 g Protein; 75 mg Sodium

Pictured above and on page 169.

Chili Corn, page 125

Chili Corn

Entertain and amaze your guests by barbecuing this fresh corn, husks and all. Served with a spicy butter, your dinner companions will enjoy your ingenuity. Use preshucked corn wrapped in foil when it is not in season.

Corncobs, in husks	4	4
Water		
Butter, melted	1/4 cup	60 mL
Chili powder	1/2 tsp.	2 mL
Garlic powder	1/2 tsp.	2 mL
Ground cumin	1/2 tsp.	2 mL

Soak corncobs in water for about 1 hour until husks are soaked through. Preheat gas barbecue to medium. Cook cobs on ungreased grill for 25 to 30 minutes, turning occasionally, until corn is tender (see Note). Let stand for about 5 minutes until cool enough to handle.

Combine remaining 4 ingredients in small cup. Peel cobs. Brush with butter mixture. Makes 4 corncobs.

1 corncob: *254 Calories; 14.5 g Total Fat (3.0 g Mono, 0.5 g Poly, 8.2 g Sat); 30 mg Cholesterol; 27 g Carbohydrate; 7 g Fibre; 5 g Protein; 95 mg Sodium*

Pictured on pages 57 and 124.

Note: Husks will appear blackened but will not affect flavour of corn.

Variation: Peel corncobs. Place cobs on separate squares of foil. Brush with butter mixture. Sprinkle 1 tbsp. (15 mL) water over each. Wrap tightly in foil. Cook on ungreased grill for 20 to 25 minutes, turning occasionally, until tender.

Tip: *Chipotle chili peppers are smoked jalapeño peppers. Be sure to wash your hands after handling. To store any leftover chipotle chili peppers, divide into recipe-friendly portions and freeze, with sauce, in airtight containers for up to one year.*

Chipotle Red Pepper Soup

Mild smoky heat and bright citrus accents in a smooth roasted red pepper soup.

Olive (or cooking) oil	1 tsp.	5 mL
Chopped onion	1 cup	250 mL
Garlic cloves, minced (or 1/2 tsp., 2 mL, powder)	2	2
Chopped chipotle peppers in adobo sauce (see Tip, this page)	1 tsp.	5 mL
Prepared vegetable broth	2 1/2 cups	625 mL
Jar of roasted red peppers (with liquid)	14 oz.	398 mL
Granulated sugar	2 tsp.	10 mL
Half-and-half cream	1/2 cup	125 mL
Grated orange zest	1 tsp.	5 mL
Salt	1/2 tsp.	2 mL
Pepper	1/4 tsp.	1 mL

Heat olive oil in large saucepan on medium. Add next 3 ingredients. Cook, uncovered, for 5 to 10 minutes, stirring occasionally, until onion is softened.

Add next 3 ingredients. Stir. Bring to a boil. Reduce heat to medium-low. Simmer, uncovered, for 5 minutes to blend flavours. Carefully process with hand blender or in blender until smooth (see Safety Tip).

Add remaining 4 ingredients. Stir. Makes about 4 3/4 cups (1.2 L). Serves 6.

1 serving: *148 Calories; 3.4 g Total Fat (1.3 g Mono, 0.2 g Poly, 1.6 g Sat); 8 mg Cholesterol; 19 g Carbohydrate; 1 g Fibre; 4 g Protein; 1061 mg Sodium*

Pictured below.

Safety Tip: Follow blender manufacturer's instructions for hot liquids. If in doubt, we recommend using a hand blender.

Top: Chipotle Red Pepper Soup, above
Bottom: Cheddar Crisps, page 80

Peas And Bacon, below

Peas And Bacon

Peas become a prominent and tantalizing part of your meal when they're mixed with bacon and red onions.

Chopped bacon slices (about 6 oz., 170 g)	1 cup	250 mL
Finely chopped red onion	1/2 cup	125 mL
Garlic clove, minced (or 1/4 tsp., 1 mL, powder)	1	1
Prepared chicken broth	1/3 cup	75 mL
Frozen peas	6 cups	1.5 L
Pepper	1/4 tsp.	1 mL

Cook first 3 ingredients in large frying pan for 5 to 10 minutes, stirring occasionally, until bacon is crisp. Transfer with slotted spoon to paper towel-lined plate to drain. Drain and discard drippings from pan. Wipe pan with paper towels.

Measure broth into same frying pan. Bring to a boil. Add peas and pepper. Cook, covered, for 5 to 8 minutes until peas are tender. Drain. Add bacon mixture. Stir. Makes about 4 1/2 cups (1.1 L). Serves 6.

1 serving: 309 Calories; 16.5 g Total Fat (7.9 g Mono, 2.1 g Poly, 5.6 g Sat); 38 mg Cholesterol; 22 g Carbohydrate; 7 g Fibre; 19 g Protein; 954 mg Sodium

Pictured above.

Herb Cheese Tortellini

Sweet red peppers and tangy balsamic dressing coat these colourful cheese-stuffed tortellini. Serve hot or at room temperature with grilled beef or chicken.

Water	12 cups	3 L
Salt	1 1/2 tsp.	7 mL
Package of fresh 3-colour cheese-filled tortellini	12 1/2 oz.	350 g
Cooking oil	1 tbsp.	15 mL
Coarsely chopped red pepper	1 1/2 cups	375 mL
Balsamic vinegar	2 tbsp.	30 mL
Sun-dried tomato pesto	2 tbsp.	30 mL
Salt	1/4 tsp.	1 mL
Pepper	1/4 tsp.	1 mL
Chopped fresh dill (or 3/4 tsp., 4 mL, dried)	1 tbsp.	15 mL
Chopped fresh parsley (or 3/4 tsp., 4 mL, flakes)	1 tbsp.	15 mL
Crumbled feta cheese	3/4 cup	175 mL

Combine water and salt in Dutch oven. Bring to a boil. Add tortellini. Boil, uncovered, for 8 to 10 minutes, stirring occasionally, until tender but firm. Drain, reserving 2 tbsp. (30 mL) cooking water. Set aside.

Heat cooking oil in large frying pan on medium. Add red pepper. Cook for 2 to 4 minutes until red pepper is tender-crisp.

Add vinegar. Heat and stir for 30 seconds.

Add next 3 ingredients and reserved cooking water. Stir. Remove from heat.

Add dill, parsley and tortellini. Toss. Sprinkle with feta. Toss. Makes about 5 cups (1.25 L). Serves 6.

1 serving: 210 Calories; 10.1 g Total Fat (2.2 g Mono, 0.9 g Poly, 4.7 g Sat); 26 mg Cholesterol; 21 g Carbohydrate; 2 g Fibre; 9 g Protein; 672 mg Sodium

Caramelized Onion Sweet Potato Soup

This sweet, velvety soup is simple to prepare but has such sophisticated and rich flavours. Your guests will never guess how easy it is to make.

Butter (or hard margarine)	1/4 cup	60 mL
Coarsely chopped onion	4 cups	1 L
Brown sugar, packed	1 tbsp.	15 mL
Coarsely chopped fresh peeled orange-fleshed sweet potato (about 1 lb., 454 g)	3 cups	750 mL
Prepared chicken broth	3 cups	750 mL
Dry sherry	1 tbsp.	15 mL
Dried thyme	1/4 tsp.	1 mL
Ground allspice	1/4 tsp.	1 mL
Salt	1/8 tsp.	0.5 mL
Pepper	1/4 tsp.	1 mL

Melt butter in large saucepan on medium. Add onion and brown sugar. Cook, uncovered, for about 30 minutes, stirring occasionally, until onion is caramelized.

Add remaining 7 ingredients. Stir. Bring to a boil. Reduce heat to medium-low. Simmer, covered, for about 20 minutes, stirring occasionally, until sweet potato is tender. Carefully process with hand blender or in blender until smooth (see Safety Tip). Makes about 5 cups (1.25 L). Serves 4.

1 serving: 270 Calories; 12.5 g Total Fat (3.3 g Mono, 0.9 g Poly, 7.5 g Sat); 30 mg Cholesterol; 37 g Carbohydrate; 5 g Fibre; 4 g Protein; 1301 mg Sodium

Pictured on page 25 and below.

Safety Tip: Follow blender manufacturer's instructions for hot liquids. If in doubt, we recommend using a hand blender.

Caramelized Onion Sweet Potato Soup, above

Saffron Risotto

Saffron, although a little expensive, is definitely worth it in this beautiful, golden risotto.

Prepared chicken broth	5 cups	1.25 L
Saffron threads (or turmeric), just a pinch		
Butter (or hard margarine)	2 tbsp.	30 mL
Arborio rice	1 1/2 cups	375 mL
Dry (or alcohol-free) white wine	1/2 cup	125 mL
Grated fresh Parmesan cheese	1/2 cup	125 mL
Pepper	1/8 tsp.	0.5 mL

Combine broth and saffron in medium saucepan. Bring to a boil. Reduce heat to low. Cover to keep hot.

Melt butter in large saucepan on medium-low. Add rice. Heat and stir for about 2 minutes until rice is coated.

Add wine. Heat and stir until wine is almost absorbed. Add 1/2 cup (125 mL) hot broth, stirring constantly until broth is almost absorbed. Repeat with remaining hot broth, 1/2 cup (125 mL) at a time, until broth is absorbed and rice is tender.

Add cheese and pepper. Stir. Makes about 5 cups (1.25 L). Serves 6.

1 serving: 291 Calories; 7.8 g Total Fat (2.1 g Mono, 0.5 g Poly, 4.2 g Sat); 17 mg Cholesterol; 47 g Carbohydrate; 1 g Fibre; 8 g Protein; 1419 mg Sodium

Stuffed Pasta Shells, page 129

Stuffed Pasta Shells

These elegant pasta shells are packed with a creamy ricotta filling and nestled in a rich cream sauce topped with golden crumbs—need we say more?

Water	10 cups	2.5 L
Salt	1 1/4 tsp.	6 mL
Jumbo shell pasta	24	24
Ricotta cheese	2 cups	500 mL
Sun-dried tomato pesto	1/3 cup	75 mL
PARMESAN CREAM SAUCE		
Butter (or hard margarine)	2 tbsp.	30 mL
Finely chopped onion	1/4 cup	60 mL
All-purpose flour	3 tbsp.	50 mL
Milk	3 cups	750 mL
Grated Parmesan cheese	1/2 cup	125 mL
Ground nutmeg	1/8 tsp.	0.5 mL
Pepper, sprinkle		
CRUMB TOPPING		
Crushed Ritz crackers (about 20 crackers)	3/4 cup	175 mL
Finely chopped fresh basil	2 tbsp.	30 mL

Combine water and salt in Dutch oven or large pot. Bring to a boil. Add pasta. Boil, uncovered, for about 15 minutes, stirring occasionally, until tender but firm. Drain. Rinse with cold water. Drain well. Set aside.

Combine ricotta cheese and pesto in medium bowl. Set aside.

Parmesan Cream Sauce: Melt butter in medium saucepan on medium. Add onion. Cook, uncovered, for about 5 minutes, stirring often, until softened.

Add flour. Heat and stir for 1 minute.

Slowly add 1 cup (250 mL) milk, stirring constantly until boiling and thickened. Add remaining milk. Cook and stir until heated through.

Add next 3 ingredients. Stir. Remove from heat. Add 1/2 cup (125 mL) to ricotta mixture. Pour remaining sauce into ungreased 9 x 13 inch (22 x 33 cm) baking dish. Spread evenly. Spoon about 2 tbsp. (30 mL) ricotta mixture into each pasta shell. Arrange in single layer over sauce in baking dish. Bake, covered, in 325°F (160°C) oven for about 30 minutes until heated through.

Crumb Topping: Sprinkle cracker crumbs over shells. Bake, uncovered, for about 15 minutes until sauce is bubbling around edges.

Sprinkle with basil. Makes 24 stuffed shells. Serves 12.

1 serving: 295 Calories; 13.3 g Total Fat (4.6 g Mono, 0.4 g Poly, 7.8 g Sat); 37 mg Cholesterol; 25 g Carbohydrate; 1 g Fibre; 18 g Protein; 586 mg Sodium

Pictured on pages 61 and 128.

Lemon Garlic-Dressed Greens, below

Lemon Garlic–Dressed Greens

Vibrant tender-crisp vegetables are marinated in Asian-inspired flavours for a personality-packed side.

Water	12 cups	3 L
Salt	1 tsp.	5 mL
Sugar snap peas, trimmed	3/4 lb.	340 g
Fresh (or frozen) whole green beans	3 cups	750 mL
Sliced red pepper	2 cups	500 mL
GARLIC PEPPER DRESSING		
Orange juice	3 tbsp.	50 mL
Soy sauce	2 tbsp.	30 mL
Rice vinegar	1 tbsp.	15 mL
Sesame oil (for flavour)	1 tbsp.	15 mL
Liquid honey	1 tsp.	5 mL
Garlic powder	1/2 tsp.	2 mL
Pepper	1/2 tsp.	2 mL
Grated lemon zest	1 tbsp.	15 mL

Combine water and salt in Dutch oven or large pot. Bring to a boil. Add next 3 ingredients. Reduce heat to medium. Boil gently, uncovered, for 3 to 5 minutes until vegetables are tender-crisp. Drain. Rinse with cold water. Drain well. Transfer to large bowl.

Garlic Pepper Dressing: Whisk all 8 ingredients in small bowl. Makes about 1/2 cup (125 mL) dressing. Drizzle over vegetables. Toss until coated. Let stand, covered, for 30 minutes to blend flavours. Makes about 8 cups (2 L). Serves 12.

1 serving: 51 Calories; 1.3 g Total Fat (0.5 g Mono, 0.5 g Poly, 0.2 g Sat); 0 mg Cholesterol; 8 g Carbohydrate; 3 g Fibre; 2 g Protein; 137 mg Sodium

Pictured on pages 64, 65 and above.

Vegetable Bulgur, below

Spiced Almond Couscous

Cumin and cinnamon-infused couscous makes a perfect side for roast chicken or pork.

Prepared chicken broth	3 cups	750 mL
Butter (or hard margarine)	2 tbsp.	30 mL
Lemon juice	1 tbsp.	15 mL
Ground cinnamon	1/4 tsp.	1 mL
Ground cumin	1/4 tsp.	1 mL
Paprika	1/4 tsp.	1 mL
Couscous	2 cups	500 mL
Raisins	1/3 cup	75 mL
Sliced natural almonds, toasted (see Tip, page 79)	3 tbsp.	50 mL

Combine first 6 ingredients in large saucepan. Bring to a boil. Add couscous and raisins. Stir. Remove from heat. Let stand, covered, for 5 minutes. Fluff with fork.

Add almonds. Stir. Makes about 6 cups (1.5 L). Serves 6.

1 serving: 330 Calories; 7.1 g Total Fat (2.7 g Mono, 1.0 g Poly, 2.8 g Sat); 10 mg Cholesterol; 57 g Carbohydrate; 4 g Fibre; 10 g Protein; 777 mg Sodium

Vegetable Bulgur

This wholesome side of whole-grain goodness and colourful vegetables is laced with the delicate flavours of ginger and lemon.

Prepared chicken broth	1 1/2 cups	375 mL
Bulgur	1 cup	250 mL
Cooking oil	1 tsp.	5 mL
Chopped onion	1 cup	250 mL
Finely grated gingerroot	2 tsp.	10 mL
Garlic clove, minced (or 1/4 tsp., 1 mL, powder)	1	1
Diced red pepper	1 cup	250 mL
Diced zucchini (with peel)	1 cup	250 mL
Dried oregano	1/2 tsp.	2 mL
Salt	1/4 tsp.	1 mL
Pepper	1/8 tsp.	0.5 mL
Grated lemon zest	2 tsp.	10 mL

Measure broth into medium saucepan. Bring to a boil. Add bulgur. Stir. Reduce heat to medium. Boil gently, covered, for 3 to 5 minutes, without stirring, until liquid is almost absorbed. Remove from heat. Let stand, covered, for 10 minutes. Fluff with fork. Cover to keep warm.

Heat cooking oil in Dutch oven on medium. Add next 3 ingredients. Cook, uncovered, for 5 to 10 minutes, stirring often, until onion is softened.

Add next 5 ingredients. Cook, uncovered, for 5 to 8 minutes, stirring often, until vegetables are tender-crisp.

Add lemon zest and bulgur. Stir. Makes about 4 cups (1 L). Serves 6.

1 serving: 115 Calories; 1.5 g Total Fat (0.6 g Mono, 0.5 g Poly, 0.2 g Sat); 0 mg Cholesterol; 23 g Carbohydrate; 4 g Fibre; 4 g Protein; 476 mg Sodium

Pictured on page 13 and above.

Chili Raspberry Greens

A refreshing raspberry dressing with a subtle heat makes crisp salad greens an adventure in dining.

CHILI RASPBERRY VINAIGRETTE

Raspberry jam	2 tbsp.	30 mL
Red wine vinegar	1 1/2 tbsp.	25 mL
Lime juice	1 tbsp.	15 mL
Dijon mustard	1 tsp.	5 mL
Dried crushed chilies	1/4 tsp.	1 mL
Salt	1/8 tsp.	0.5 mL
Pepper	1/8 tsp.	0.5 mL
Olive oil	3 tbsp.	50 mL

SALAD

Spring mix lettuce, lightly packed	4 cups	1 L
Sliced fresh white mushrooms	1 cup	250 mL
Thinly sliced red pepper	1 cup	250 mL
Cherry tomatoes, halved	8	8

Chili Raspberry Vinaigrette: Whisk first 7 ingredients in small bowl until smooth. Slowly add olive oil, stirring constantly with whisk until combined. Makes about 1/2 cup (125 mL) vinaigrette.

Salad: Put all 4 ingredients into large bowl. Drizzle with Chili Raspberry Vinaigrette. Toss. Makes about 8 cups (2 L). Serves 4.

1 serving: 146 Calories; 10.4 g Total Fat (7.5 g Mono, 1.0 g Poly, 1.4 g Sat); 0 mg Cholesterol; 13 g Carbohydrate; 2 g Fibre; 2 g Protein; 100 mg Sodium

Pictured below.

Chili Raspberry Greens, above

Spicy Rice Noodles

These vibrant yellow rice noodles have an Asian flavour and a lingering chili heat. Serve with grilled pork or chicken.

Dry sherry	2 tbsp.	30 mL
Fish sauce	2 tbsp.	30 mL
Lime juice	2 tbsp.	30 mL
Soy sauce	2 tbsp.	30 mL
Brown sugar, packed	1 tbsp.	15 mL
Turmeric	1/4 tsp.	1 mL
Package of rice stick noodles	9 oz.	250 g
Boiling water		
Cooking oil	1 tbsp.	15 mL
Finely chopped onion	1/2 cup	125 mL
Chili paste (sambal oelek)	1 tsp.	5 mL
Finely grated gingerroot (or 1/4 tsp., 1 mL, ground ginger)	1 tsp.	5 mL
Garlic clove, minced (or 1/4 tsp., 1 mL, powder)	1	1
Fresh bean sprouts	1 cup	250 mL
Snow peas, trimmed and halved	3/4 cup	175 mL
Thinly sliced red pepper	1/2 cup	125 mL
Chopped fresh cilantro or parsley	1 tbsp.	15 mL

Combine first 6 ingredients in small cup. Set aside.

Put noodles into large heatproof bowl. Cover with boiling water. Let stand for about 20 minutes until softened. Drain. Set aside.

Heat large frying pan or wok on medium-high until very hot. Add cooking oil. Add onion. Stir-fry for 1 to 2 minutes until onion starts to soften.

Add next 3 ingredients. Heat and stir for 1 minute.

Add next 3 ingredients. Stir-fry for 1 minute. Add noodles and soy sauce mixture. Stir-fry for 1 to 2 minutes until heated through.

Sprinkle with cilantro. Makes about 4 cups (1 L). Serves 4.

1 serving: 337 Calories; 4.1 g Total Fat (2.2 g Mono, 1.2 g Poly, 0.4 g Sat); 0 mg Cholesterol; 68 g Carbohydrate; 3 g Fibre; 6 g Protein; 1228 mg Sodium

Veggie Chow Mein, page 133

Veggie Chow Mein

This refreshing chow mein is packed with tender-crisp veggies and fresh egg noodles.

Chinese dried mushrooms	8	8
Boiling water	1 cup	250 mL
Water	12 cups	3 L
Fresh, thin Chinese-style egg noodles	10 1/2 oz.	300 g
Sesame (or cooking) oil	2 tsp.	10 mL
Cooking oil	1 tbsp.	15 mL
Fresh bean sprouts	2 cups	500 mL
Sugar snap peas, trimmed	2 cups	500 mL
Grated carrot	1 cup	250 mL
Canned, sliced bamboo shoots, drained	1/2 cup	125 mL
Chopped green onion	1/3 cup	75 mL
Dry sherry	3 tbsp.	50 mL
Oyster sauce	3 tbsp.	50 mL
Soy sauce	3 tbsp.	50 mL
Granulated sugar	1 tsp.	5 mL
Sesame seeds, toasted (see Tip, page 79), optional	1 tsp.	5 mL

Put mushrooms into small heatproof bowl. Add boiling water. Stir. Let stand for about 20 minutes until softened. Drain. Remove and discard stems. Slice thinly. Set aside.

Measure water into Dutch oven or large pot. Bring to a boil. Add noodles. Boil, uncovered, for about 1 minute until tender but firm. Drain. Rinse with cold water. Drain well. Return to same pot. Add sesame oil. Toss. Set aside.

Heat wok or large frying pan on medium-high until very hot. Add cooking oil. Add next 4 ingredients. Stir-fry for about 2 minutes until vegetables are tender-crisp.

Add green onion. Stir. Add next 4 ingredients. Stir. Add noodles. Stir-fry for about 1 minute until heated through.

Sprinkle with sesame seeds. Makes about 7 1/2 cups (1.9 L). Serves 8.

1 serving: 237 Calories; 4.5 g Total Fat (1.5 g Mono, 1.5 g Poly, 0.7 g Sat); 38 mg Cholesterol; 39 g Carbohydrate; 4 g Fibre; 10 g Protein; 364 mg Sodium

Pictured on pages 52 and 132.

Pistachio Pilaf, below

Pistachio Pilaf

This versatile rice and pistachio side is infused with mild licorice flavour from fennel. If you can't find shelled pistachios, use toasted slivered almonds.

Prepared chicken broth	2 cups	500 mL
Paprika	1/4 tsp.	1 mL
Long grain white rice	1 cup	250 mL
Olive (or cooking) oil	1 tbsp.	15 mL
Finely chopped fennel bulb	3/4 cup	175 mL
Diced red pepper	1/2 cup	125 mL
Finely chopped onion	1/2 cup	125 mL
Chopped pistachios	1/3 cup	75 mL
Chopped fresh parsley (or 3/4 tsp., 4 mL, flakes)	1 tbsp.	15 mL

Combine broth and paprika in medium saucepan. Bring to a boil. Add rice. Stir. Reduce heat to medium-low. Simmer, covered, for 15 minutes, without stirring. Remove from heat. Let stand, covered, for about 5 minutes until liquid is absorbed and rice is tender. Fluff with fork.

Heat olive oil in medium frying pan on medium. Add next 3 ingredients. Cook for about 5 minutes, stirring often, until vegetables are tender. Add to rice.

Add pistachios and parsley. Toss. Makes about 4 cups (1 L). Serves 6.

1 serving: 215 Calories; 6.3 g Total Fat (3.6 g Mono, 1.4 g Poly, 0.9 g Sat); 0 mg Cholesterol; 35 g Carbohydrate; 3 g Fibre; 5 g Protein; 521 mg Sodium

Pictured above.

Double-Done Stuffed Potatoes

The creamy filling of these double-done potatoes in crisp potato shells is satisfying to the extreme.

Large unpeeled baking potatoes	4	4
Sour cream	3/4 cup	175 mL
Chopped green onion	1/4 cup	60 mL
Grated Parmesan cheese	1/4 cup	60 mL
Mayonnaise	2 tbsp.	30 mL
Dijon mustard	2 tsp.	10 mL
Prepared horseradish	2 tsp.	10 mL
Garlic powder	1/2 tsp.	2 mL
Salt	1/2 tsp.	2 mL
Dried thyme, just a pinch		
Cooking spray		
Paprika, sprinkle		

Prick potatoes in several places with fork. Wrap individually with paper towel. Microwave on high (100%) for 15 to 20 minutes, turning at halftime, until tender. Let stand until cool enough to handle. Cut potatoes in half lengthwise. Carefully scoop pulp from potatoes into medium bowl, leaving about 1/4 inch (6 mm) thick shells. Mash potato pulp.

Add next 9 ingredients. Mash.

Spray outsides of potato shells with cooking spray. Arrange on ungreased baking sheet with sides. Spoon potato mixture into shells.

Sprinkle with paprika. Bake in 400°F (205°C) oven for about 20 minutes until hot and golden. Serves 8.

1 serving: 269 Calories; 10.4 g Total Fat (3.6 g Mono, 0.9 g Poly, 5.5 g Sat); 22 mg Cholesterol; 34 g Carbohydrate; 3 g Fibre; 11 g Protein; 497 mg Sodium

Coleslaw, below

Coleslaw

This sweet and tangy coleslaw with dill pickles is a crowd-pleaser with family-friendly flavours.

Coleslaw mix	3 cups	750 mL
Finely chopped red onion	1/4 cup	60 mL
Finely chopped dill pickle	2 tbsp.	30 mL
Sliced green onion	2 tbsp.	30 mL

BUTTERMILK DRESSING		
Buttermilk	3 tbsp.	50 mL
Mayonnaise	2 tbsp.	30 mL
Granulated sugar	1 tbsp.	15 mL
Dill pickle juice	1 1/2 tsp.	7 mL
Prepared mustard	1 tsp.	5 mL
Salt	1/8 tsp.	0.5 mL
Cayenne pepper, sprinkle		

Put first 4 ingredients into medium bowl. Toss.

Buttermilk Dressing: Combine all 7 ingredients in small bowl. Makes about 1/3 cup (75 mL) dressing. Add to coleslaw mixture. Toss until coated. Makes about 4 cups (1 L). Serves 4.

1 serving: 74 Calories; 3.8 g Total Fat (2.0 g Mono, 1.3 g Poly, 0.3 g Sat); 2 mg Cholesterol; 10 g Carbohydrate; 2 g Fibre; 1 g Protein; 222 mg Sodium

Pictured above.

Asian Noodle Vegetable Soup

This light gingery broth with tender noodles and a flavourful mix of vegetables is a perfect complement for an Asian-inspired evening. Feel free to add some chili paste, such as sambal oelek, if you like a little more heat.

Prepared chicken broth	6 cups	1.5 L
Can of baby corn, drained and sliced	14 oz.	398 mL
Sliced fresh white mushrooms	1 cup	250 mL
Thinly sliced carrot	1 cup	250 mL
Soy sauce	1 tbsp.	15 mL
Finely grated gingerroot (or 1/2 tsp., 2 mL, ground ginger)	2 tsp.	10 mL
Garlic clove, minced (or 1/4 tsp., 1 mL, powder)	1	1
Coarsely chopped baby bok choy, lightly packed	2 cups	500 mL
Rice stick noodles, broken up	1 1/2 cups	375 mL
Chopped green onion	1/4 cup	60 mL
Sesame oil (for flavour)	2 tsp.	10 mL

Combine first 7 ingredients in large saucepan or Dutch oven. Bring to a boil.

Add next 3 ingredients. Bring to a boil. Reduce heat to medium. Boil gently, uncovered, for about 5 minutes until noodles are tender.

Add sesame oil. Stir. Makes about 8 cups (2 L). Serves 6.

1 serving: 297 Calories; 3.0 g Total Fat (1.1 g Mono, 1.1 g Poly, 0.6 g Sat); 0 mg Cholesterol; 59 g Carbohydrate; 7 g Fibre; 7 g Protein; 2015 mg Sodium

Chili Tapenade Toasts

Olives abound in this colourful tapenade with a dash of chili heat. Makes a great alternative to dinner rolls or garlic bread. Serve as an appetizer or a side.

CHILI TAPENADE

Olive oil	1/2 tsp.	2 mL
Chopped onion	1 cup	250 mL
Garlic cloves, minced (or 1/2 tsp., 2 mL, powder)	2	2
Chili paste (sambal oelek)	1/4 tsp.	1 mL
Salt	1/4 tsp.	1 mL
Pepper	1/4 tsp.	1 mL
Chopped red pepper	1 cup	250 mL
Slivered almonds, toasted (see Tip, page 79)	1 cup	250 mL
Can of diced green chilies	4 oz.	113 g
Chopped pitted black olives	1/4 cup	60 mL
Olive oil	1 tbsp.	15 mL

TOAST

Olive oil	1 tsp.	5 mL
French bread slices, 1/2 inch (12 mm) thick	4	4

Chili Tapenade: Heat first amount of olive oil in medium frying pan. Add next 5 ingredients. Cook for 5 to 10 minutes, stirring occasionally, until onion is softened.

Add red pepper. Cook for about 2 minutes, stirring occasionally, until tender-crisp. Transfer to food processor.

Add next 3 ingredients. With motor running, add second amount of olive oil in thin stream through feed chute until mixture is coarsely ground but spreadable. Makes about 2 1/2 cups (625 mL) tapenade.

Toast: Brush olive oil on bread slices. Arrange on ungreased baking sheet. Bake in 400°F (205°C) oven for 3 to 5 minutes until golden. Spread about 1 tbsp. (15 mL) tapenade on toasted sides of bread. Bake for about 5 minutes until heated through. Store remaining tapenade in an airtight container in the freezer for up to 1 month. Cut toasts in half. Serves 4.

1 serving: 105 Calories; 2.2 g Total Fat (1.3 g Mono, 0.3 g Poly, 0.4 g Sat); 0 mg Cholesterol; 18 g Carbohydrate; 1 g Fibre; 3 g Protein; 212 mg Sodium

Pictured on page 33 and below.

Honey Basil Asparagus, below

Honey Basil Asparagus

These tender asparagus spears are lightly dressed in a subtly sweet and tangy basil vinaigrette. A simple yet superb side.

Salt	1/2 tsp.	2 mL
Fresh asparagus, trimmed of tough ends	1 lb.	454 g

HONEY BASIL VINAIGRETTE

Olive (or cooking) oil	1/4 cup	60 mL
Apple cider vinegar	2 tbsp.	30 mL
Chopped fresh basil (or 1 1/2 tsp., 6 mL, dried)	1 tbsp.	15 mL
Grated Parmesan cheese	1 tbsp.	15 mL
Liquid honey	1 tbsp.	15 mL
Dry mustard	1 tsp.	5 mL
Salt	1/8 tsp.	0.5 mL

Pour water into large frying pan until about 1 inch (2.5 cm) deep. Add salt. Bring to a boil. Add asparagus. Reduce heat to medium. Boil gently for 3 to 5 minutes until tender-crisp. Drain. Transfer to serving plate.

Honey Basil Vinaigrette: Combine all 7 ingredients in jar with tight-fitting lid. Shake well. Makes about 1/2 cup (125 mL) vinaigrette. Drizzle over asparagus. Serves 4.

1 serving: 205 Calories; 15.9 g Total Fat (10.8 g Mono, 1.2 g Poly, 3.3 g Sat); 6 mg Cholesterol; 10 g Carbohydrate; 3 g Fibre; 6 g Protein; 257 mg Sodium

Pictured above.

Chili Tapenade Toasts, above

Spicy Confetti Salad, page 137

Spicy Confetti Salad

This colourful combination of black beans and vegetables is showcased to perfection in a fresh basil dressing.

Can of black beans, rinsed and drained	19 oz.	540 mL
Can of kernel corn, drained	12 oz.	341 mL
Finely chopped red pepper	1 cup	250 mL
Finely chopped green onion	1/4 cup	60 mL

BASIL DRESSING

Fresh basil leaves	1/4 cup	60 mL
Olive oil	3 tbsp.	50 mL
Red wine vinegar	3 tbsp.	50 mL
Chopped jalapeño pepper (see Tip, page 101)	2 tsp.	10 mL
Granulated sugar	1/2 tsp.	2 mL
Salt	1/2 tsp.	2 mL
Pepper	1/2 tsp.	2 mL

Combine first 4 ingredients in medium bowl.

Basil Dressing: Put all 7 ingredients into blender. Process until smooth. Makes about 1/3 cup (75 mL) dressing. Drizzle over bean mixture. Toss. Makes about 4 1/2 cups (1.1 L). Serves 6.

1 serving: 172 Calories; 6.8 g Total Fat (5.0 g Mono, 0.6 g Poly, 0.9 g Sat); 0 mg Cholesterol; 26 g Carbohydrate; 6 g Fibre; 5 g Protein; 733 mg Sodium

Pictured on page 136.

Tip: *Don't get caught red handed! Wear rubber gloves when handling beets.*

Smashed Baby Potatoes, below

Citrus-Glazed Beets

There's nothing like fresh beets— especially when they're coated with a buttery, orange glaze.

Diced fresh peeled beets (see Tip, this page)	3 cups	750 mL
Frozen concentrated orange juice	2 tbsp.	30 mL
Lemon juice	2 tbsp.	30 mL
Butter (or hard margarine)	1 tbsp.	15 mL
Granulated sugar	1 tbsp.	15 mL
Cornstarch	1 1/2 tsp.	7 mL
Salt	1/4 tsp.	1 mL

Pour water into medium saucepan until about 1 inch (2.5 cm) deep. Add beets. Cover. Bring to a boil. Reduce heat to medium. Boil gently for about 30 minutes, covered, until tender. Drain. Transfer to small bowl. Cover to keep warm.

Combine remaining 6 ingredients in same saucepan. Heat and stir on medium until boiling and thickened. Add beets. Stir until coated. Makes about 3 cups (750 mL). Serves 6.

1 serving: 67 Calories; 2.0 g Total Fat (0.5 g Mono, 0.1 g Poly, 1.2 g Sat); 5 mg Cholesterol; 12 g Carbohydrate; 2 g Fibre; 1 g Protein; 164 mg Sodium

Variation: Use 2 cans (14 oz., 398 mL, each) cooked beets instead of fresh beets. Omit cooking.

Smashed Baby Potatoes

Rustically prepared with skins and all, these crisp little potatoes present a worthy alternative to traditionally roasted potatoes.

Baby potatoes	3 lbs.	1.4 kg
Butter (or hard margarine)	1/4 cup	60 mL
Pepper	1/4 tsp.	1 mL
Butter (or hard margarine), melted	1 tbsp.	15 mL
Seasoned salt	1/2 tsp.	2 mL

Pour water into Dutch oven until 1 inch (2.5 cm) deep. Add first 3 ingredients. Cover. Bring to a boil. Reduce heat to medium. Boil gently, for 12 to 15 minutes until potatoes are tender. Drain. Arrange potatoes in single layer on 2 greased baking sheets with sides. Press potatoes flat with bottom of cup or bowl.

Brush with melted butter. Sprinkle with seasoned salt. Broil on centre and upper racks in oven for 8 to 10 minutes, switching position of baking sheets at halftime, until browned and crisp. Serves 12.

1 serving: 102 Calories; 1.0 g Total Fat (0.3 g Mono, trace Poly, 0.6 g Sat); 3 mg Cholesterol; 20 g Carbohydrate; 1 g Fibre; 3 g Protein; 72 mg Sodium

Pictured on page 64 and above.

Orange-Glazed Vegetables, page 139

Orange-Glazed Vegetables

When getting ready for a dinner party, it's nice to free up some oven space and use your slow cooker to full advantage. Especially when the outcome is tender carrots and sweet potatoes coated in spiced orange glaze. Use orange-fleshed sweet potatoes for best results.

Baby carrots	1 lb.	454 g
Fresh, peeled orange-fleshed sweet potatoes, cut into 1 1/2 inch (3.8 cm) cubes	2 1/2 lbs.	1.1 kg
Chopped dried apricot	1 cup	250 mL
Maple (or maple-flavoured) syrup	1/2 cup	125 mL
Frozen concentrated orange juice	1/4 cup	60 mL
Water	1/4 cup	60 mL
Butter (or hard margarine), melted	2 tbsp.	30 mL
Salt	1/4 tsp.	1 mL
Pepper	1/4 tsp.	1 mL
Ground allspice	1/8 tsp.	0.5 mL
Water	1 tbsp.	15 mL
Cornstarch	2 tsp.	10 mL

Layer first 3 ingredients, in order given, in 4 quart (4 L) slow cooker.

Combine next 7 ingredients in small bowl. Pour over apricot. Cook, covered, on Low for 6 hours or High for 3 hours. Transfer vegetables to serving bowl with slotted spoon. Transfer liquid to small saucepan. Bring to a boil.

Stir second amount of water into cornstarch in small cup. Add to liquid. Heat and stir until boiling and thickened. Pour over vegetables. Makes about 8 cups (2 L). Serves 12.

1 serving: 171 Calories; 2.3 g Total Fat (0.5 g Mono, 0.3 g Poly, 1.3 g Sat); 5 mg Cholesterol; 37 g Carbohydrate; 4 g Fibre; 2 g Protein; 111 mg Sodium

Pictured on pages 61 and 138.

Apple Walnut Quinoa

Sweet and spicy, this unusual side dish of toasted walnuts, apples, peppers and irresistibly light quinoa (KEEN-wah) complements almost any entree.

Prepared vegetable broth	1 1/2 cups	375 mL
Quinoa, rinsed and drained	1 cup	250 mL
Olive (or cooking) oil	1 tsp.	5 mL
Chopped onion	1 cup	250 mL
Garlic clove, minced (or 1/4 tsp., 1 mL, powder)	1	1
Chopped peeled cooking apple (such as McIntosh)	1 cup	250 mL
Chopped red pepper	1/2 cup	125 mL
Finely diced fresh hot chili pepper (see Tip, page 101)	2 tsp.	10 mL
Chopped walnuts, toasted (see Tip, page 79)	1/4 cup	60 mL
Balsamic vinegar	3 tbsp.	50 mL
Liquid honey	2 tbsp.	30 mL
Pepper	1/4 tsp.	1 mL

Measure broth into medium saucepan. Bring to a boil. Add quinoa. Stir. Reduce heat to medium-low. Simmer, covered, for about 20 minutes, without stirring, until quinoa is tender and liquid is absorbed.

Heat olive oil in large frying pan on medium. Add onion and garlic. Cook for 5 to 10 minutes, stirring often, until onion is softened.

Add next 3 ingredients. Cook for about 2 minutes, stirring occasionally, until red pepper starts to soften.

Add walnuts and quinoa. Stir.

Combine remaining 3 ingredients in small cup. Drizzle over quinoa mixture. Toss until coated. Makes about 4 cups (1 L). Serves 4.

1 serving: 311 Calories; 8.8 g Total Fat (2.2 g Mono, 4.7 g Poly, 0.9 g Sat); 0 mg Cholesterol; 52 g Carbohydrate; 6 g Fibre; 8 g Protein; 188 mg Sodium

Pictured on page 25 and below.

Apple Walnut Quinoa, above

Braised Carrots And Leeks, page 141

Braised Carrots And Leeks

This subtle side is a superb accompaniment for stew, salmon or roasted meats. Use a crinkle cutter on the carrots for an interesting presentation.

Cooking oil	1 tbsp.	15 mL
Chopped leek (white part only), see Note	3 cups	750 mL
Sliced carrot (1/2 inch, 12 mm, thick)	3 cups	750 mL
Dry (or alcohol-free) white wine	1/4 cup	60 mL
Water	1/4 cup	60 mL
Bay leaf	1	1
Chopped fresh mint	1 tsp.	5 mL
Granulated sugar	1 tsp.	5 mL
Salt	1/2 tsp.	2 mL
Pepper	1/4 tsp.	1 mL
Butter (or hard margarine)	1 tbsp.	15 mL
Chopped fresh mint	2 tsp.	10 mL

Heat cooking oil in large frying pan on medium. Add leek and carrot. Cook for 5 minutes, stirring occasionally.

Add next 7 ingredients. Stir. Bring to a boil. Reduce heat to medium-low. Cook, covered, for about 10 minutes until carrot is tender. Cook, uncovered, for 2 to 4 minutes until liquid is almost evaporated.

Add butter. Toss. Transfer to serving bowl. Sprinkle with second amount of mint. Makes about 4 cups (1 L). Serves 6.

1 serving: 104 Calories; 4.5 g Total Fat (1.8 g Mono, 0.9 g Poly, 1.4 g Sat); 5 mg Cholesterol; 14 g Carbohydrate; 3 g Fibre; 1 g Protein; 264 mg Sodium

Pictured on page 140.

Note: To wash leeks thoroughly, cut in half lengthwise first.

Honey Lime Sourdough Salad

With seasoned sourdough croutons, your guests will get an unexpected treat in this sweet and crisp salad.

Olive oil	1 tbsp.	15 mL
Ground cumin	1/2 tsp.	2 mL
Salt	1/4 tsp.	1 mL
Pepper	1/4 tsp.	1 mL
Sourdough bread cubes, 1/2 inch (12 mm)	3 cups	750 mL
Spring mix lettuce, lightly packed	3 cups	750 mL
Sliced fresh white mushrooms	1 cup	250 mL
Chopped yellow pepper	1 cup	250 mL
Cherry tomatoes, cut in half	10	10
HONEY LIME DRESSING		
Lime juice	3 tbsp.	50 mL
Liquid honey	3 tbsp.	50 mL
Olive oil	2 tbsp.	30 mL
Sesame oil (for flavour)	2 tsp.	10 mL
Dijon mustard	1 tsp.	5 mL
Grated lime zest	1 tsp.	5 mL
Dried crushed chilies	1/2 tsp.	2 mL
Salt	1/4 tsp.	1 mL
Pepper	1/8 tsp.	0.5 mL

Whisk first 4 ingredients in medium bowl. Add bread cubes. Toss until coated. Arrange in single layer on baking sheet with sides. Bake in 350°F (175°C) oven for about 5 minutes, stirring at halftime, until starting to turn golden. Let stand for 10 minutes.

Combine next 4 ingredients in large bowl. Add bread cubes.

Honey Lime Dressing: Combine all 9 ingredients in jar with tight-fitting lid. Shake well. Makes about 2/3 cup (150 mL) dressing. Drizzle over bread mixture. Toss. Makes about 8 cups (2 L). Serves 6.

1 serving: 213 Calories; 8.8 g Total Fat (5.6 g Mono, 1.3 g Poly, 1.2 g Sat); 0 mg Cholesterol; 30 g Carbohydrate; 2 g Fibre; 4 g Protein; 366 mg Sodium

Pictured below.

Honey Lime Sourdough Salad, above

Carrot And Beet Salad, below

Carrot And Beet Salad

The vibrant colours and bright flavours make this a pretty and delicious side to go with any main course.

DRESSING		
Olive oil	1/4 cup	60 mL
Lemon juice	3 tbsp.	50 mL
Liquid honey	2 tbsp.	30 mL
Salt	1/4 tsp.	1 mL
Pepper	1/4 tsp.	1 mL

SALAD		
Coarsely grated carrot	2 cups	500 m
Can of whole baby beets, drained and diced (see Tip, page 137)	14 oz.	398 mL
Chopped fresh mint	2 tsp.	10 mL

Dressing: Whisk all 5 ingredients in small bowl until smooth. Makes about 2/3 cup (150 mL) dressing.

Salad: Put carrot and beet into medium bowl. Toss. Drizzle with dressing. Toss until coated.

Sprinkle with mint. Makes about 4 cups (1 L). Serves 6.

1 serving: 140 Calories; 9.2 g Total Fat (6.7 g Mono, 0.8 g Poly, 1.2 g Sat); 0 mg Cholesterol; 15 g Carbohydrate; 2 g Fibre; 1 g Protein; 251 mg Sodium

Pictured above.

Roasted Raisin Nut Broccoli

Be prepared to receive many compliments from your dinner companions with this unusual combination of raisins, sun-dried tomatoes, maple syrup and broccoli.

Broccoli florets	6 cups	1.5 L
Sun-dried tomatoes, softened in boiling water for 10 minutes before chopping	1/4 cup	60 mL
Raisins	1/3 cup	75 mL
Chopped fresh sage (or 1/2 tsp., 2 mL, dried)	2 tsp.	10 mL
Salt	1/2 tsp.	2 mL
Pepper	1/4 tsp.	1 mL
Maple (or maple-flavoured) syrup	3 tbsp.	50 mL
Butter (or hard margarine), melted	2 tbsp.	30 mL
Pine nuts, toasted (see Tip, page 79)	1/4 cup	60 mL

Put broccoli into greased 9 x 13 inch (22 x 33 cm) baking dish. Sprinkle with next 5 ingredients.

Combine maple syrup and melted butter in small cup. Drizzle over broccoli. Stir until coated. Cover with foil. Bake in 400°F (205°C) oven for 20 to 25 minutes until broccoli is tender.

Sprinkle with pine nuts. Makes about 5 cups (1.25 L). Serves 6.

1 serving: 151 Calories; 7.6 g Total Fat (2.3 g Mono, 1.7 g Poly, 3.0 g Sat); 10 mg Cholesterol; 20 g Carbohydrate; 4 g Fibre; 4 g Protein; 290 mg Sodium

Tip: *When baking or broiling food in a frying pan with a handle that isn't ovenproof, wrap the handle in foil and keep it to the front of the oven, away from the element.*

Dressed-Up Roasted Vegetables

Dressed up with pecans and a balsamic drizzle, roasted vegetables have never been done better.

Pecan pieces	1/3 cup	75 mL
Bag of frozen Brussels sprouts, larger ones cut in half	1 lb.	500 g
Sliced parsnip (1/4 inch, 6 mm thick)	1 cup	250 mL
Large red onion, cut into 1/2 inch (12 mm) wedges	1	1
Butter (or hard margarine), melted	3 tbsp.	50 mL
Cooking oil	2 tbsp.	30 mL
Salt	1 tsp.	5 mL
Olive oil	3 tbsp.	50 mL
Balsamic vinegar	2 tbsp.	30 mL
Dijon mustard	1 tsp.	5 mL
Garlic clove, minced (or 1/4 tsp., 1 mL, powder)	1	1
Grated lemon zest	1/2 tsp.	2 mL
Salt	1/4 tsp.	1 mL
Pepper	1/4 tsp.	1 mL

Put first 4 ingredients into large bowl. Add next 3 ingredients. Toss until coated. Spread evenly on greased baking sheet with sides. Bake in 450°F (230°C) oven for about 20 minutes, stirring at halftime, until browned and tender. Transfer to serving bowl.

Combine remaining 7 ingredients in small cup. Drizzle over vegetables. Toss until coated. Makes about 6 cups (1.5 L). Serves 6.

1 serving: 257 Calories; 22.1 g Total Fat (11.8 g Mono, 3.7 g Poly, 5.3 g Sat); 15 mg Cholesterol; 14 g Carbohydrate; 4 g Fibre; 4 g Protein; 551 mg Sodium

Pictured on page 16 and below.

Dressed-Up Roasted Vegetables, above

Rustic Frying Pan Potatoes

The appearance may be rustic but the taste is pure gourmet when crisp potato layers are packed with caramelized onion, bacon and cheese.

Bacon slices, diced	4	4
Sliced onions	1 1/2 cups	375 mL
Unpeeled potatoes, cut in half lengthwise and cut crosswise into 1/4 inch (6 mm) thick slices	1 1/2 lbs.	680 g
Prepared chicken broth	1 cup	250 mL
Pepper	1/2 tsp.	2 mL
Grated mozzarella cheese	1 cup	250 mL
Chopped fresh chives	2 tbsp.	30 mL

Cook bacon in large frying pan on medium until crisp. Transfer to paper towel-lined plate to drain.

Heat 1 tbsp. (15 mL) drippings in same frying pan. Add onion. Cook for 5 to 10 minutes, stirring often, until golden. Transfer to small bowl.

Arrange half of potato in single layer in same frying pan. Arrange onion and half of bacon over top. Arrange remaining potato over bacon.

Pour broth over potato mixture. Sprinkle with pepper and remaining bacon. Bring to a boil. Reduce heat to medium-low. Simmer, covered, for about 20 minutes, without stirring, until potato is tender.

Sprinkle with cheese. Broil on top rack in oven for about 5 minutes until cheese is melted and golden (see Tip, page 142).

Sprinkle with chives. Serves 8.

1 serving: 140 Calories; 5.7 g Total Fat (2.2 g Mono, 0.4 g Poly, 2.8 g Sat); 16 mg Cholesterol; 19 g Carbohydrate; 2 g Fibre; 7 g Protein; 312 mg Sodium

Anise Crème Brulée, page 145

Anise Crème Brulée

Velvety white chocolate and subtle licorice flavours give a delicious twist to this classic dessert.

Whipping cream	1 1/3 cups	325 mL
Star anise	2	2
White chocolate baking squares (1 oz., 28 g, each), chopped	4	4
Granulated sugar	3 tbsp.	50 mL
Egg yolks (large), fork-beaten	4	4
Vanilla extract	1/4 tsp.	1 mL
Granulated sugar	2 tbsp.	30 mL

Place four 1/2 cup (125 mL) ovenproof ramekins in ungreased 9 x 9 inch (22 x 22 cm) baking dish. Combine cream and star anise in small heavy saucepan. Heat on medium, stirring occasionally, until bubbles form around edge of saucepan. Remove from heat. Let stand, covered, for 5 minutes. Remove and discard star anise.

Add chocolate and first amount of sugar. Stir until chocolate is melted.

Add egg yolks and vanilla. Whisk until well combined. Pour into ramekins. Carefully pour boiling water into baking dish until halfway up sides of ramekins. Bake in 300°F (150°C) oven for about 45 minutes until custard is set along edges but centre still wobbles. Carefully remove ramekins from water. Place on wire rack to cool completely. Chill, covered, for about 4 hours until cold.

Sprinkle second amount of sugar evenly over top of each. Broil on top rack in oven for about 3 minutes until sugar is bubbling and browned. Let stand for 5 minutes. Serves 4.

1 serving: 537 Calories; 42.8 g Total Fat (10.2 g Mono, 1.7 g Poly, 24.9 g Sat); 297 mg Cholesterol; 33 g Carbohydrate; 0 g Fibre; 6 g Protein; 65 mg Sodium

Pictured on pages 2, 25 and 144.

Brandied Cherry Brownies, below

Brandied Cherry Brownies

These dense, fudge-filled brownies get the gourmet treatment with a liberal helping of a dashing brandied cherry sauce.

Bittersweet chocolate baking squares (1 oz., 28 g, each), chopped	2	2
Butter (or hard margarine)	1/2 cup	125 mL
Large eggs	2	2
Granulated sugar	3/4 cup	175 mL
All-purpose flour	1/3 cup	75 mL
Cocoa, sifted if lumpy	1/4 cup	60 mL
BRANDIED CHERRY SAUCE		
Cornstarch	2 tsp.	10 mL
Can of pitted Bing cherries in light syrup (with syrup)	14 oz.	398 mL
Brandy	2 tbsp.	30 mL

Brownies: Heat chocolate and butter in small heavy saucepan on lowest heat, stirring often, until chocolate is almost melted. Do not overheat. Remove from heat. Stir until smooth.

Beat eggs in medium bowl until frothy. Add sugar and chocolate mixture. Stir until combined.

Add flour and cocoa. Stir until just moistened. Spread evenly in greased 9 x 9 inch (22 x 22 cm) baking pan. Bake in 350°F (175°C) oven for about 25 minutes until wooden pick inserted in centre comes out moist but not wet with batter. Do not overbake. Let stand in pan on wire rack for 5 minutes. Cuts into 6 pieces. Place brownies on 6 dessert plates.

Brandied Cherry Sauce: Stir cornstarch into 1 tbsp. (15 mL) syrup from cherries. Heat cherries and remaining syrup in small saucepan on medium for about 5 minutes, stirring occasionally, until bubbling. Stir cornstarch mixture. Add to saucepan. Heat and stir until boiling and thickened.

Add brandy. Stir. Makes about 1 cup (250 mL) sauce. Spoon over brownies. Serves 6.

1 serving: 398 Calories; 21.3 g Total Fat (4.8 g Mono, 0.8 g Poly, 12.3 g Sat); 102 mg Cholesterol; 50 g Carbohydrate; 2 g Fibre; 5 g Protein; 134 mg Sodium

Pictured above.

Tiger Butter Bark

Amaze your guests with this simple but impressive-looking dessert. Smooth, creamy peanut butter and chocolate will make them purr with satisfaction.

White chocolate melting wafers	6 cups	1.5 L
Smooth peanut butter	1 cup	250 mL
Semi-sweet chocolate baking squares (1 oz., 28 g, each), coarsely chopped	2	2

Heat melting wafers and peanut butter in medium heavy saucepan on lowest heat, stirring often, until almost melted. Do not overheat. Remove from heat. Stir until smooth. Spread evenly on waxed paper-lined 11 X 17 inch (28 x 43 cm) baking sheet with sides.

Put chocolate into small microwave-safe bowl. Microwave, uncovered, on medium (50%) for 20 to 30 seconds at a time, stirring in between, until chocolate is almost melted. Do not overheat. Stir until smooth. Transfer to small resealable freezer bag. Snip tiny piece off 1 corner. Drizzle chocolate over peanut butter mixture in zigzag pattern. Swirl knife through mixture to create marbled effect. Chill for about 30 minutes until set. Remove from pan. Remove and discard waxed paper. Break bark into irregular-shaped pieces, about 1 1/2 x 4 inches (3.8 x 10 cm) each. Makes about 28 pieces.

1 piece: 261 Calories; 17.0 g Total Fat (5.6 g Mono, 1.6 g Poly, 8.4 g Sat); 8 mg Cholesterol; 25 g Carbohydrate; 1 g Fibre; 5 g Protein; 34 mg Sodium

Pictured on page 49, at left and on page 176.

Tiger Butter Bark, right

Bumbleberry Crisp

With a fresh mixture of strawberries, blueberries and rhubarb topped with a crunchy oat and nut topping, this homey treat is bound to pull at the heartstrings. Serve with whipped cream or ice cream.

Chopped fresh (or frozen) strawberries	3 cups	750 mL
Chopped peeled cooking apple (such as McIntosh)	2 cups	500 mL
Fresh (or frozen) blueberries	2 cups	500 mL
Chopped fresh (or frozen) rhubarb	1 cup	250 mL
Brown sugar, packed	1/2 cup	125 mL
Apple juice	1/3 cup	75 mL
Almond liqueur	3 tbsp.	50 mL
Minute tapioca	3 tbsp.	50 mL
Ground cinnamon	1/2 tsp.	2 mL
ALMOND OAT TOPPING		
Large flake rolled oats	1 1/2 cups	375 mL
All-purpose flour	3/4 cup	175 mL
Brown sugar, packed	1/2 cup	125 mL
Butter (or hard margarine), melted	1/2 cup	125 mL
Whole natural almonds, chopped and toasted (see Tip, page 79)	1/2 cup	125 mL
Almond extract	1/2 tsp.	2 mL
Ground cinnamon	1/2 tsp.	2 mL

Combine first 9 ingredients in large bowl. Transfer to greased 2 quart (2 L) baking dish.

Almond Oat Topping: Combine all 7 ingredients in medium bowl. Sprinkle over fruit mixture. Press down gently. Bake in 350°F (175°C) oven for 45 to 50 minutes until topping is golden and fruit mixture is bubbling. Makes about 7 cups (1.75 L).

1 cup (250 mL): 516 Calories; 19.6 g Total Fat (6.6 g Mono, 1.9 g Poly, 8.6 g Sat); 34 mg Cholesterol; 79 g Carbohydrate; 6 g Fibre; 8 g Protein; 107 mg Sodium

Pictured on pages 57, 68 and below.

Bumbleberry Crisp, above

Cinnamon Ginger Oranges, below

Cinnamon Ginger Oranges

For a light and unique dessert, sweet oranges are gently cooked in a light ginger and cinnamon-infused syrup. Serve at room temperature or cold. Goes great with Baklava Rosettes, page 153.

Granulated sugar	1 1/2 cups	375 mL
Water	1 cup	250 mL
Gingerroot slices, 1/4 inch (6 mm) thick	2	2
Cinnamon stick (4 inches, 10 cm)	1	1
Large oranges, peeled and segmented (see Tip, page 113)	4	4

Combine first 4 ingredients in large saucepan. Heat and stir on medium until sugar is dissolved.

Add orange. Cook, uncovered, for 5 minutes to blend flavours. Remove and discard gingerroot and cinnamon stick. Divide orange segments into 6 dessert bowls. Pour about 3 tbsp. (50 mL) sugar mixture over each serving. Serves 6.

1 serving: 245 Calories; 0.2 g Total Fat (trace Mono, trace Poly, trace Sat); 0 mg Cholesterol; 63 g Carbohydrate; 3 g Fibre; 1 g Protein; trace Sodium

Pictured on page 13 and above.

Sweet Chili Fruit Galette

Sometimes the most unexpected ingredient makes a dish shine and so it is here. Sweet chili is a delicious surprise in this fruit-filled pastry.

Package of puff pastry (14 oz., 397 g), thawed according to package directions	1/2	1/2
Spreadable cream cheese, softened	1/4 cup	60 mL
Frozen mixed berries, thawed and drained	2 cups	500 mL
Granulated sugar	1/3 cup	75 mL
Sweet chili sauce	1/4 cup	60 mL
All-purpose flour	2 tbsp.	30 mL
Minute tapioca	1 tbsp.	15 mL
Dried crushed chilies	1/4 tsp.	1 mL
Can of sliced peaches in juice, drained	14 oz.	398 mL
Sweet chili sauce	2 tbsp.	30 mL
Large egg, fork-beaten	1	1

Roll out puff pastry on lightly floured surface to 11 inch (28 cm) diameter circle. Transfer to greased baking sheet.

Spread cream cheese over pastry, leaving 3 inch (7.5 cm) border.

Combine next 6 ingredients in small bowl. Spoon over cream cheese.

Combine peach slices and second amount of chili sauce in small bowl. Arrange over berry mixture. Fold a section of border up and over edge of filling. Repeat with next section, allowing pastry to overlap so that fold is created. Pinch to seal. Repeat until pastry border is completely folded around filling.

Brush pastry with egg. Bake in 375°F (190°C) oven for about 40 minutes until pastry is puffed and golden. Cuts into 8 wedges.

1 wedge: 284 Calories; 12.7 g Total Fat (6.4 g Mono, 1.4 g Poly, 4.2 g Sat); 31 mg Cholesterol; 40 g Carbohydrate; 3 g Fibre; 4 g Protein; 454 mg Sodium

Pictured on page 33 and at left.

Sweet Chili Fruit Galette, right

Coconut Lime Tart

The unexpected chocolate coconut crumb crust makes this lime confection a deliciously tart show-stopper.

COCONUT CRUMB CRUST

Chocolate wafer crumbs	2 cups	500 mL
Butter (or hard margarine), melted	1/2 cup	125 mL
Medium sweetened coconut	1/2 cup	125 mL

LIME CURD

Granulated sugar	1 cup	250 mL
Lime juice	1/2 cup	125 mL
Butter (or hard margarine)	1/3 cup	75 mL
Large eggs, fork-beaten	4	4
Medium sweetened coconut	1 cup	250 mL
Grated lime zest	1 tsp.	5 mL
Frozen whipped topping, thawed	2 cups	500 mL

Coconut Crumb Crust: Combine all 3 ingredients in medium bowl. Press firmly in bottom and 1 inch (2.5 cm) up side of greased 9 inch (22 cm) springform pan. Chill for 20 minutes.

Lime Curd: Whisk first 3 ingredients in medium saucepan on medium for 3 to 5 minutes until sugar is dissolved. Remove from heat.

Whisk eggs in medium bowl until frothy. Slowly add lime mixture, stirring constantly with whisk. Return to saucepan. Heat and stir on medium for 2 to 4 minutes until mixture is thick enough to coat back of spoon. Do not boil.

Stir in coconut and lime zest. Transfer to medium bowl. Cover with plastic wrap directly on surface to prevent skin from forming. Chill for about 2 hours until cooled completely. Makes about 2 1/2 cups (625 mL) curd.

Fold in whipped topping. Spread evenly in crust. Freeze for about 3 hours until firm. Cuts into 8 wedges.

1 wedge: 538 Calories; 33.8 g Total Fat (7.5 g Mono, 2.3 g Poly, 21.9 g Sat); 144 mg Cholesterol; 57 g Carbohydrate; 2 g Fibre; 6 g Protein; 373 mg Sodium

Pictured below.

Sake Mellowed Melon, below

Sake Mellowed Melon

This adult dessert features various types of melon marinated in a sweet honey and sake (pronounced SAH-kee) mixture. Zen dining at its finest!

Cubed cantaloupe (3/4 inch, 2 cm, pieces)	3 cups	750 mL
Cubed honeydew (3/4 inch, 2 cm, pieces)	2 cups	500 mL
Cubed watermelon (3/4 inch, 2 cm, pieces)	2 cups	500 mL
Sake (rice wine)	1 cup	250 mL
Apple juice	1/2 cup	125 mL
Liquid honey	1/3 cup	75 mL

Put first 3 ingredients into large bowl.

Combine remaining 3 ingredients in small bowl. Pour over melon mixture. Toss gently. Chill, covered, for 1 hour. Makes about 5 1/2 cups (1.4 L). Serves 8.

1 serving: 137 Calories; 0.2 g Total Fat (0 g Mono, 0.1 g Poly, 0.1 g Sat); 0 mg Cholesterol; 27 g Carbohydrate; 1 g Fibre; 1 g Protein; 20 mg Sodium

Pictured on page 53 and above.

Coconut Lime Tart, above

Ginger Almond Trifle, page 151

Ginger Almond Trifle

This traditional dessert is always a crowd-pleaser. The addition of crystallized ginger is a pleasant surprise that combines well with the almond liqueur.

GINGER CUSTARD

Whole (or 2%) milk	2 cups	500 mL
Gingerroot slices, 1/4 inch (6 mm) thick	3	3
Egg yolks (large)	5	5
Granulated sugar	1/2 cup	125 mL
Reserved strawberry syrup	1/2 cup	125 mL
Cornstarch	1/4 cup	60 mL
Almond liqueur	1 tsp.	5 mL

TRIFLE

Can of sliced peaches in juice, drained and juice reserved, chopped	28 oz.	796 mL
Container of frozen sliced strawberries in light syrup, thawed, drained and syrup reserved	15 oz.	425 g
Can of pineapple tidbits, drained and juice reserved	14 oz.	398 mL
Reserved peach juice	1/2 cup	125 mL
Reserved pineapple juice	1/2 cup	125 mL
Minced crystallized ginger	1/4 cup	60 mL
Cognac	2 tbsp.	30 mL
Almond liqueur	1 tbsp.	15 mL
Angel food cake (10 inch, 25 cm, diameter), cut into 1 inch (2.5 cm) cubes	1	1
Whipping cream	1 cup	250 mL
Sliced natural almonds, toasted (see Tip, page 79)	1/2 cup	125 mL
Sliced crystallized ginger	1/4 cup	60 mL

Ginger Custard: Combine milk and gingerroot in medium saucepan. Heat on medium, stirring occasionally until hot, but not boiling. Reduce heat to medium-low. Cook, uncovered, for about 3 minutes, stirring occasionally. Remove and discard gingerroot.

Whisk next 4 ingredients in medium bowl. Slowly add hot milk mixture, stirring constantly with whisk. Return to saucepan. Heat and stir on medium for 3 to 5 minutes until thickened.

Add liqueur. Stir. Transfer to medium bowl. Cover with plastic wrap directly on surface to prevent skin from forming. Place in large bowl of ice water. Cool for 30 minutes, stirring often. Chill for about 30 minutes until cold. Makes about 3 1/3 cups (825 mL) custard.

Trifle: Combine first 8 ingredients in separate medium bowl.

To assemble, layer ingredients in large glass serving bowl as follows:

1. Half of cake cubes
2. Half of fruit mixture
3. Half of Ginger Custard, spread evenly
4. Remaining cake cubes
5. Remaining fruit mixture
6. Remaining Ginger Custard, spread evenly

Beat whipping cream in small bowl until soft peaks form. Spread evenly over top. Sprinkle with almonds and ginger. Chill for 4 hours to blend flavours. Makes about 16 cups (4 L). Serves 12.

1 serving: 439 Calories; 13.7 g Total Fat (5.3 g Mono, 1.5 g Poly, 6.1 g Sat); 110 mg Cholesterol; 73 g Carbohydrate; 2 g Fibre; 8 g Protein; 298 mg Sodium

Pictured on pages 65 and 150.

Buttery Toffee Popcorn, below

Buttery Toffee Popcorn

Punch up the pizazz on your traditional movie night munchies with this mind-blowing toffee popcorn. You won't be able to put it down!

Popped corn (1/2 cup, 125 mL, unpopped)	16 cups	4 L
Brown sugar, packed	2 cups	500 mL
Butter	1 cup	250 mL
White corn syrup	1/2 cup	125 mL
Salt	1 tsp.	5 mL
Baking soda	1 tsp.	5 mL

Put popped corn into large roasting pan. Set aside.

Combine next 4 ingredients in medium saucepan. Heat and stir, on medium, until butter is melted and sugar is dissolved. Bring to a boil over medium-high heat. Boil uncovered for 5 minutes, without stirring. Remove from heat.

Add baking soda. Stir well. Pour over popcorn. Stir until coated. Bake, uncovered, in 200°F (95°C) oven for about 1 hour, stirring often, until popcorn is glazed and crunchy. Spread evenly on waxed paper. Let stand until dry. Makes about 16 cups (4 L).

1 cup (250 mL): 254 Calories; 11.6 g Total Fat (2.9 g Mono, 0.4 g Poly, 7.2 g Sat); 30 mg Cholesterol; 39 g Carbohydrate; 1 g Fibre; 1 g Protein; 332 mg Sodium

Pictured on page 49 and above.

Peaches And Cream Slice

This chilled, light-textured dessert has delicate and mellow peach and rum flavours. Perfect for a gentle end to the evening.

Can of sliced peaches in syrup (with syrup)	14 oz.	398 mL
Rum extract	1/4 tsp.	1 mL
Can of sliced peaches in syrup (with syrup)	14 oz.	398 mL
Can of sweetened condensed milk	11 oz.	300 mL
Block of cream cheese, softened	8 oz.	250 g
Rum extract	1/2 tsp.	2 mL
Large eggs	5	5

Put first amount of peaches with syrup and extract into blender or food processor. Process until smooth. Transfer to small bowl. Cover. Set aside.

Put second amount of peaches with syrup into blender or food processor. Process until smooth. Add remaining 4 ingredients. Process until smooth. Line 9 inch (22 cm) deep dish pie plate with greased foil. Place in ovenproof pan (such as a broiler pan) large enough to hold pie plate. Pour cream cheese mixture into pie plate. Pour hot water into pan until halfway up side of pie plate. Bake in 325°F (160°C) oven for about 45 minutes until knife inserted in centre comes out clean. Remove to wire rack. Cool completely. Chill, covered, for at least 4 hours. Run knife around inside edge of pie plate to loosen. Place large serving plate upside down over pie plate. Invert. Remove pie plate. Spoon reserved peach mixture over individual servings. Cuts into 10 wedges.

1 wedge: 251 Calories; 13.1 g Total Fat (4.1 g Mono, 0.8 g Poly, 7.5 g Sat); 128 mg Cholesterol; 27 g Carbohydrate; 1 g Fibre; 8 g Protein; 140 mg Sodium

Pictured at left.

Peaches And Cream Slice, right

Baklava Rosettes

Individual rosettes of baklava make for a lively and luscious dessert. Bake only as many as you need—the pastries can be made, placed on a baking sheet or tray and then put in the freezer. Once frozen, store in airtight containers in the freezer. Bake from frozen for about 30 minutes.

Finely chopped unsalted mixed nuts	3 cups	750 mL
Dark raisins	1 1/2 cups	375 mL
Liquid honey	2/3 cup	150 mL
Ground cinnamon	1 tsp.	5 mL
Ground cumin	1 tsp.	5 mL
Phyllo pastry sheets, thawed according to package directions	18	18
Butter, melted	1 cup	250 mL
Granulated sugar	2 tbsp.	30 mL
Ground cinnamon	1/2 tsp.	2 mL
Ground ginger	1/2 tsp.	2 mL
Liquid honey, warmed	3 tbsp.	50 mL

Combine nuts and raisins in small bowl. Combine next 3 ingredients in small cup. Drizzle over nut mixture. Stir until coated.

Lay 1 pastry sheet on work surface, with longest side closest to you. Keep remaining sheets covered with damp towel to prevent drying. Brush top half of sheet with melted butter. Fold bottom half up and over top half. Brush with melted butter. Spread 1/4 cup (60 mL) nut mixture along bottom of pastry sheet, leaving a 1 inch (2.5 cm) edge on both sides. Fold up, jelly-roll style, from bottom. Twist several times while coiling loosely into a 4 inch (10 cm) circle. Tuck end under. Place on greased baking sheet. Brush with melted butter. Repeat with remaining pastry sheets, butter and nut mixture.

Combine next 3 ingredients in small bowl. Sprinkle over pastries. Bake in 350°F (175°C) oven for 20 to 25 minutes until golden.

Brush with honey. Makes 18 rosettes.

1 rosette: 381 Calories; 23.1 g Total Fat (10.4 g Mono, 3.0 g Poly, 8.3 g Sat); 27 mg Cholesterol; 41 g Carbohydrate; 3 g Fibre; 6 g Protein; 168 mg Sodium

Pictured below.

Baklava Rosettes, above

Lime Mango Sorbet, below

Lime Mango Sorbet

The dynamic taste of homemade sorbet is always appreciated—and the combination of mango and lime is exceptional and refreshing.

Can of sliced mango in syrup (with syrup)	14 oz.	398 mL
Frozen concentrated limeade	1/2 cup	125 mL
Half-and-half cream	1/2 cup	125 mL
Grated lime zest	2 tsp.	10 mL
Rum extract	1 tsp.	5 mL

Put mango with syrup into blender or food processor. Process until smooth.

Add remaining 4 ingredients. Process until smooth. Spread evenly in plastic wrap-lined 9 x 5 x 3 inch (22 x 12.5 x 7.5 cm) loaf pan. Freeze for about 4 hours until firm. Remove from pan. Cut into 4 squares. Cut squares diagonally to make 8 triangles. Serve immediately. Serves 4.

1 serving: 189 Calories; 3.7 g Total Fat (1.1 g Mono, 0.1 g Poly, 2.3 g Sat); 12 mg Cholesterol; 41 g Carbohydrate; 1 g Fibre; 1 g Protein; 16 mg Sodium

Pictured on page 23 and above.

Pumpkin Pecan Pound Cake

This moist pumpkin pound cake with crunchy pecans is made spectacular with a smooth caramel brandy sauce.

Butter (or hard margarine)	1 cup	250 mL
Granulated sugar	2 cups	500 mL
Large eggs	4	4
Can of pure pumpkin (no spices)	14 oz.	398 mL
Vanilla extract	2 tsp.	10 mL
All-purpose flour	3 cups	750 mL
Baking powder	2 tsp.	10 mL
Baking soda	1 tsp.	5 mL
Ground cinnamon	1 tsp.	5 mL
Ground allspice	1/2 tsp.	2 mL
Salt	1/4 tsp.	1 mL
Chopped pecans, toasted (see Tip, page 79)	1 cup	250 mL

BRANDY SAUCE

Brown sugar, packed	1/2 cup	125 mL
Butter	1/3 cup	75 mL
Half-and-half cream	1/2 cup	125 mL
Brandy	2 tbsp.	30 mL

Cream butter and sugar in large bowl. Add eggs, 1 at a time, beating well after each addition. Add pumpkin and vanilla in 2 additions, beating well after each addition. Mixture may look slightly curdled.

Combine next 6 ingredients in medium bowl. Slowly add to pumpkin mixture, beating on low until combined. Fold in pecans. Spread evenly in greased and floured 12 cup (3 L) bundt pan. Bake in 350°F (175°C) oven for about 60 minutes until wooden pick inserted in centre of cake comes out clean. Let stand in pan for 10 minutes. Invert onto wire rack to cool slightly.

Brandy Sauce: Combine sugar and butter in small saucepan. Heat and stir on medium until boiling. Boil gently, uncovered, for about 5 minutes, without stirring, until slightly thickened. Remove from heat.

Add cream and brandy. Stir. Makes about 1 cup (250 mL) sauce. Drizzle over individual servings. Cake cuts into 12 slices.

1 slice with 4 tsp. (20 mL) sauce:
563 Calories; 30.2 g Total Fat (10.3 g Mono, 3.2 g Poly, 14.7 g Sat); 119 mg Cholesterol; 68 g Carbohydrate; 2 g Fibre; 7 g Protein; 371 mg Sodium

Pictured at left.

Pumpkin Pecan Pound Cake, right

Coconut Custard Pie

Silky coconut custard in a flaky pastry puts any diner's coconut cream pie to shame. A pure delight to eat.

Unbaked 9 inch (22 cm) deep dish pie shell	1	1
Egg white (large), fork-beaten	1	1
Medium sweetened coconut, toasted (see Tip, page 79)	3 tbsp.	50 mL
Half-and-half cream	1 cup	250 mL
Milk	1/2 cup	125 mL
Egg yolk (large)	1	1
Large eggs	2	2
Granulated sugar	1/3 cup	75 mL
Coconut extract	1 tsp.	5 mL
Vanilla extract	1/2 tsp.	2 mL
Salt	1/4 tsp.	1 mL

Prick pie shell all over with fork. Bake in 400°F (205°C) oven for about 10 minutes until golden. Remove from oven.

Immediately brush egg white over pie shell. Bake for another 2 minutes.

Place pie shell on ungreased baking sheet (see Note). Sprinkle coconut evenly in bottom of pie shell. Cover outside edges of pastry with strips of foil. Set aside.

Heat cream and milk in small saucepan on medium, stirring occasionally, until bubbles form around edge of saucepan.

Whisk remaining 6 ingredients in medium bowl. Slowly add milk mixture, stirring constantly with whisk. Pour into pie shell. Bake in 350°F (175°C) oven for 20 minutes. Remove strips of foil. Bake for about 15 minutes until knife inserted in centre comes out clean. Transfer to wire rack. Cool for 2 hours. Cuts into 8 wedges.

1 wedge: 237 Calories; 13.2 g Total Fat (1.9 g Mono, 0.4 g Poly, 6.4 g Sat); 88 mg Cholesterol; 24 g Carbohydrate; trace Fibre; 5 g Protein; 221 mg Sodium

Pictured below.

Note: Placing pie shell on baking sheet provides a safe way to transfer hot pan out of oven.

Coconut Custard Pie, above

Butter Crunch Ice Cream Squares, below

Butter Crunch Ice Cream Squares

Let your dinner companions satisfy both their sweet and salt cravings with one special dessert. The salty pretzel crust holds ice cream drizzled with sweet chocolate and caramel.

CRUST

Stick pretzels, broken up	1 1/2 cups	375 mL
Butter (or hard margarine)	1/2 cup	125 mL
Brown sugar, packed	1/4 cup	60 mL

FILLING

Butterscotch ripple ice cream, softened	8 cups	2 L

TOPPING

Butterscotch ice cream topping	1/4 cup	60 mL
Chocolate ice cream topping	1/4 cup	60 mL

Crust: Put pretzels into food processor. Process until coarse crumbs form. Melt butter, covered, in medium saucepan on medium. Remove from heat. Add pretzel crumbs and sugar. Stir well. Press firmly in foil-lined 9 x 9 inch (22 x 22 cm) pan. Cool completely.

Filling: Spoon ice cream over crust. Spread evenly.

Topping: Drizzle butterscotch and chocolate ice cream topping over ice cream. Swirl with knife to create marble effect. Freeze for about 2 hours until firm. Cuts into 12 pieces.

1 piece: 447 Calories; 18.2 g Total Fat (2.2 g Mono, 0.7 g Poly, 11.6 g Sat); 53 mg Cholesterol; 64 g Carbohydrate; 1 g Fibre; 6 g Protein; 582 mg Sodium

Pictured on page 19 and above.

Pear Masala Crepes, page 157

Pear Masala Crepes

Chai-spiced pear and a cream topping makes these crepes a decadent delight worthy of any French bistro.

CARDAMOM CREPES

All-purpose flour	1 1/2 cups	375 mL
Granulated sugar	3 tbsp.	50 mL
Ground cardamom	1/2 tsp.	2 mL
Salt	1/2 tsp.	2 mL
Large eggs	4	4
Milk	1 1/2 cups	375 mL
Cooking oil	1 tbsp.	15 mL
Cooking oil	2 tsp.	10 mL

TOPPING

Can of sweetened condensed milk	11 oz.	300 mL
Vanilla pudding powder	2 tbsp.	30 mL
Ground cardamom	1/4 tsp.	1 mL
Ground cinnamon	1/4 tsp.	1 mL
Ground ginger	1/4 tsp.	1 mL
Pepper	1/8 tsp.	0.5 mL
Can of pear halves in juice, drained and diced	14 oz.	398 mL
Whipping cream	1 1/2 cups	375 mL
Sliced almonds, toasted (see Tip, page 79)	1/2 cup	125 mL

Cardamom Crepes: Combine first 4 ingredients in medium bowl. Make a well in centre.

Whisk next 3 ingredients in small bowl. Add to well. Whisk until smooth. Let stand, covered, for 1 hour.

Heat 1/4 tsp. (1 mL) of second amount of cooking oil in small (8 inch, 20 cm) non-stick frying pan on medium. Pour about 1/4 cup (60 mL) batter into pan. Immediately swirl batter to coat bottom, lifting and tilting pan to ensure entire bottom is covered. Cook until top is set and brown spots appear on bottom. Turn crepe over. Cook until brown spots appear on bottom. Transfer to plate. Repeat with remaining batter, adding more cooking oil as necessary to prevent sticking. Makes about 14 crepes.

Topping: Beat first 6 ingredients in small bowl until smooth. Add pear. Stir.

Using same beaters, beat cream in medium bowl until soft peaks form. Fold in pear mixture. Fold crepes in half, then in half again. Arrange crepes, slightly overlapping, on serving platter. Spoon topping over crepes.

Sprinkle with almonds. Serves 6.

1 serving: 313 Calories; 16.8 g Total Fat (6.5 g Mono, 1.7 g Poly, 7.7 g Sat); 95 mg Cholesterol; 35 g Carbohydrate; 2 g Fibre; 8 g Protein; 185 mg Sodium

Pictured on pages 4, 67 and 156.

Note: Crepes can be made ahead and kept at room temperature for a few hours until ready to serve. To reheat, stack crepes on a baking sheet or oven-proof platter and cover with foil. Place in 200°F (95°C) oven for about 1 hour until ready to serve. Serve topping in separate bowl.

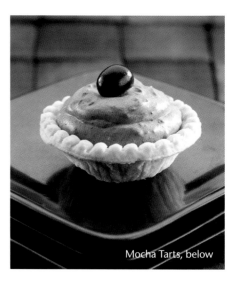

Mocha Tarts, below

Mocha Tarts

Made especially to cure your favourite coffee lover's sweet tooth, these extravagant chocolate-filled tarts are decorated with a chocolate-coated coffee bean.

Unbaked tart shells	20	20
Milk	1/2 cup	125 mL
Coffee liqueur	1/2 cup	125 mL
Box of instant chocolate fudge pudding powder (4-serving size)	1	1
Instant coffee (or espresso) granules	1 tsp.	5 mL
Whipping cream	1 cup	250 mL
Chocolate-covered coffee beans, for garnish		

Place tart shells on ungreased baking sheet. Bake in 375°F (190°C) oven for about 10 minutes until golden. Cool.

Beat next 4 ingredients in medium bowl for 2 minutes.

Beat cream in small bowl until soft peaks form. Fold into pudding mixture until no white streaks remain. Spoon into tart shells.

Garnish with coffee beans. Chill. Makes 20 tarts.

1 tart: 181 Calories; 10.6 g Total Fat (4.3 g Mono, 0.9 g Poly, 4.7 g Sat); 16 mg Cholesterol; 18 g Carbohydrate; trace Fibre; 1 g Protein; 202 mg Sodium

Pictured above.

Vanilla Spice Rice Pudding

This creamy rice pudding with the chai spices of cinnamon, cardamom and ginger will have your guests yearning for more.

Cans of evaporated milk (13 1/2 oz., 385 mL, each)	2	2
Brown sugar, packed	1/3 cup	75 mL
Vanilla bean (or 2 tsp., 10 mL, vanilla extract)	1	1
Ground cinnamon	1/2 tsp.	2 mL
Ground cardamom	1/4 tsp.	1 mL
Ground ginger	1/4 tsp.	1 mL
Salt	1/8 tsp.	0.5 mL
Large eggs	4	4
Cooked basmati (or long grain white) rice (about 1/2 cup, 125 mL, uncooked)	1 1/2 cups	375 mL
Chopped dried apricot	1/4 cup	60 mL
Chopped pitted dates	1/4 cup	60 mL
Pistachios, chopped	2 tbsp.	30 mL

Combine first 7 ingredients in large saucepan. Heat on medium for about 5 minutes, stirring occasionally, until bubbles form around edge of pan. Remove from heat. Let stand for 10 minutes. Remove vanilla bean. Split in half lengthwise. Scrape seeds from pods into milk mixture. Discard pod.

Whisk eggs in medium bowl until frothy. Slowly add milk mixture, stirring constantly with whisk. Add next 3 ingredients. Stir. Transfer to greased 8 x 8 inch (20 x 20 cm) baking dish. Place dish in ungreased 9 x 13 inch (22 x 33 cm) baking dish. Slowly pour boiling water into pan until halfway up sides of baking dish. Bake in 325°F (160°C) oven for 30 minutes. Stir. Bake for 10 to 15 minutes until knife inserted in centre of pudding comes out clean.

Sprinkle with pistachios. Serves 6.

1 serving: *312 Calories; 7.3 g Total Fat (2.9 g Mono, 1.0 g Poly, 2.7 g Sat); 134 mg Cholesterol; 47 g Carbohydrate; 2 g Fibre; 15 g Protein; 239 mg Sodium*

Pictured at left.

Vanilla Spice Rice Pudding, right

White Chocolate Lemon Tiramisu

This light and lemony dessert with white chocolate and rum makes an elegant ending to a meal. For more family-friendly flavours, omit the rum and dip the biscuits in 1/2 cup (125 mL) thawed frozen lemonade concentrate.

Butter (or hard margarine), cut up	1/2 cup	125 mL
Granulated sugar	1/2 cup	125 mL
Lemon juice	1/2 cup	125 mL
Grated lemon zest (see Tip, page 122)	1 tbsp.	15 mL
Large eggs	4	4
White chocolate baking squares (1 oz., 28 g, each), chopped	3	3
Mascarpone cheese	10 oz.	285 g
Icing (confectioner's) sugar	1/2 cup	125 mL
Dark (navy) rum	1/4 cup	60 mL
Frozen concentrated lemonade, thawed	1/4 cup	60 mL
Ladyfingers	20 – 25	20 – 25

Combine first 4 ingredients in medium saucepan. Heat and stir on medium for about 5 minutes until sugar is dissolved and butter is melted.

Whisk eggs in medium bowl until frothy. Slowly add hot lemon mixture, stirring constantly with whisk. Return to saucepan. Heat and stir on medium for 3 to 5 minutes until mixture is thick enough to coat back of spoon. Remove from heat.

Add white chocolate. Stir until melted. Transfer to medium bowl. Place in large bowl of ice water. Chill for about 30 minutes, stirring often, until cold (see Note).

Beat cheese and icing sugar in medium bowl until smooth. Add lemon mixture. Mix well.

Combine rum and concentrated lemonade in shallow bowl. Quickly dip ladyfingers into rum mixture, 1 at a time, until partially soaked through. Arrange in single layer in bottom of 9 x 9 inch (22 x 22 cm) baking dish, trimming to fit if necessary. Spread half of cheese mixture over ladyfingers. Repeat with remaining ladyfingers, rum and cheese mixture. Chill, covered, for 2 hours. Cuts into 8 pieces.

1 piece: 530 Calories; 34.7 g Total Fat (4.0 g Mono, 0.8 g Poly, 19.1 g Sat); 188 mg Cholesterol; 46 g Carbohydrate; 1 g Fibre; 8 g Protein; 192 mg Sodium

Pictured below.

Note: Place plastic wrap directly on surface of chocolate lemon curd. Chill for 1 to 2 hours until cold.

White Chocolate Lemon Tiramisu, above

Fruit Tarts

This attractive, light dessert of pudding-filled tarts decorated with fruit is simple yet superb.

Frozen, unbaked tart shells	12	12
Semi-sweet chocolate chips	1/4 cup	60 mL
Milk	1 1/2 cups	375 mL
Box of instant banana pudding powder (4-serving size)	1	1
Strawberry slices	24	24
Canned mandarin orange segments, drained and blotted dry	12	12
Green grapes	12	12
Apple jelly	1/4 cup	60 mL

Arrange tart shells on baking sheet. Bake in 375°F (190°C) oven for about 20 minutes until browned.

Immediately put 1 tsp. (5 mL) chocolate chips into bottom of each hot tart shell. Let stand for 2 minutes. Spread chocolate over bottom and up sides of tart shells using pastry brush or back of spoon. Let stand until cool.

Whisk milk and pudding powder in small bowl until thickened. Spoon into medium resealable freezer bag. Snip tiny piece off 1 corner. Pipe pudding mixture into tart shells.

Arrange next 3 ingredients over top.

Put jelly into small microwave-safe bowl. Microwave, uncovered, on high (100%) for 20 to 30 seconds until melted. Stir. Brush over fruit. Chill. Makes 12 tarts.

1 tart: 181 Calories; 7.3 g Total Fat (2.5 g Mono, 2.1 g Poly, 1.9 g Sat); 2 mg Cholesterol; 27 g Carbohydrate; trace Fibre; 2 g Protein; 184 mg Sodium

Black Forest Cherry Clafouti

This light and mildly sweet chocolate version of the traditional clafouti (pronounced kla-foo-TEE) can also be made with cherry brandy and served with whipped cream or ice cream. Sure to satisfy any sweet cravings your guests may have.

Jar of pitted sour cherries in light syrup (with syrup)	19 oz.	540 mL
Cherry liqueur	1 tbsp.	15 mL
Large eggs	3	3
Granulated sugar	1/3 cup	75 mL
Grated lemon zest	1 tsp.	5 mL
All-purpose flour	1/2 cup	125 mL
Cocoa, sifted if lumpy	2 tbsp.	30 mL
Ground nutmeg	1/8 tsp.	0.5 mL
Milk	1 cup	250 mL
Softened butter (or margarine)	1/4 cup	60 mL
Cherry liqueur	2 tbsp.	30 mL
Icing (confectioner's) sugar, sprinkle (optional)		

Combine cherries with syrup and first amount of liqueur in greased 2 quart (2 L) shallow baking dish. Spread evenly. Let stand for 30 minutes.

Whisk next 3 ingredients in large bowl until frothy.

Combine next 3 ingredients in small bowl. Add milk. Stir. Add to egg mixture. Stir well.

Add butter and second amount of liqueur. Stir until smooth. Pour over cherry mixture. Bake in 375°F (190°C) oven for about 40 minutes until lightly browned and knife inserted in centre comes out clean.

Sprinkle icing sugar over top. Serves 6.

1 serving: 286 Calories; 10.8 g Total Fat (3.3 g Mono, 0.7 g Poly, 6.0 g Sat); 116 mg Cholesterol; 41 g Carbohydrate; 2 g Fibre; 7 g Protein; 113 mg Sodium

Pictured at left.

Black Forest Cherry Clafouti, right

Berry Dream Squares

When you don't have time to fuss with fancy baking, this no-bake dessert takes the pressure off. Garnish squares with fresh blueberries for a special touch.

Chocolate wafer crumbs	2 1/4 cups	550 mL
Butter (or hard margarine), melted	1/2 cup	125 mL
Envelope of unflavoured gelatin (about 1 tbsp., 15 mL)	1/4 oz.	7 g
Cold water	1/2 cup	125 mL
Can of frozen concentrated grape juice, thawed	12 1/2 oz.	355 mL
Box of grape jelly powder (gelatin)	3 oz.	85 g
Can of blueberry pie filling	19 oz.	540 mL
Frozen blueberries, thawed	2 cups	500 mL
Whipping cream	1 cup	250 mL

Combine wafer crumbs and butter in medium bowl. Press firmly in bottom of greased 9 x 13 inch (22 x 33 cm) baking dish. Chill for 1 hour.

Sprinkle gelatin over cold water in small bowl. Let stand for 1 minute. Stir.

Put concentrated grape juice into medium saucepan. Bring to a boil. Remove from heat. Add jelly powder. Stir. Add gelatin mixture. Stir until dissolved. Add pie filling and blueberries. Stir. Chill for about 30 minutes, stirring occasionally, until partially set. Spoon half of blueberry mixture over crust. Spread evenly. Chill.

Beat cream until soft peaks form. Fold into remaining blueberry mixture. Spread evenly over blueberry mixture in pan. Chill for 2 hours. Cuts into 12 squares.

1 square: 398 Calories; 17.8 g Total Fat (5.0 g Mono, 1.4 g Poly, 10.0 g Sat); 46 mg Cholesterol; 59 g Carbohydrate; 3 g Fibre; 3 g Protein; 218 mg Sodium

Pictured on page 63 and below.

Berry Dream Squares, above

Chocolate Carrot Cake

A twist on a traditional favourite. Bittersweet chocolate is accented by a scrumptious chocolate cream cheese icing.

All-purpose flour	2 cups	500 mL
Baking powder	2 tsp.	10 mL
Baking soda	1 tsp.	5 mL
Ground ginger	1 tsp.	5 mL
Ground cinnamon	1/2 tsp.	2 mL
Salt	1/2 tsp.	2 mL
Large eggs	4	4
Brown sugar, packed	1 1/2 cups	375 mL
Cooking oil	1 1/4 cups	300 mL
Grated carrot	3 cups	750 mL
Bittersweet chocolate baking squares (1 oz., 28 g, each), finely chopped	5	5

CHOCOLATE CREAM CHEESE ICING

Semi-sweet chocolate baking squares (1 oz., 28 g, each), coarsely chopped	3	3
Butter (or hard margarine)	3 tbsp.	50 mL
Block of cream cheese, softened	4 oz.	125 g
Icing (confectioner's) sugar	3/4 cup	175 mL

Combine first 6 ingredients in small bowl.

Whisk next 3 ingredients in medium bowl until combined. Add carrot and chocolate. Stir. Add flour mixture. Stir until just moistened. Pour into greased and floured 12 cup (3 L) bundt pan. Spread evenly. Bake in 350°F (175°C) oven for about 55 minutes until wooden pick inserted in centre of cake comes out clean. Let stand in pan for 10 minutes. Invert onto wire rack set on waxed paper-lined baking sheet. Let stand for about 30 minutes until almost cooled.

Chocolate Cream Cheese Icing: Combine chocolate and butter in small saucepan. Heat and stir on lowest heat until chocolate is almost melted. Do not overheat. Remove from heat. Stir until smooth. Let stand for 15 minutes.

Beat cream cheese and icing sugar in medium bowl until light. Add chocolate mixture. Stir well. Makes about 1 1/4 cups (300 mL) icing. Spread over warm cake, allowing icing to flow down sides. Cuts into 16 pieces.

1 piece: 442 Calories; 28.2 g Total Fat (11.8 g Mono, 5.4 g Poly, 7.3 g Sat); 60 mg Cholesterol; 47 g Carbohydrate; 2 g Fibre; 5 g Protein; 258 mg Sodium

Simple Crepes Suzette, page 163

Simple Crepes Suzette

Those time-tested, traditional desserts are awe-inspiring for good reason. This simplified version eliminates the flambéing and still serves up delightful crepes with buttery orange sauce to leave your guests blissfully satisfied.

CREPES

All-purpose flour	1 1/4 cups	300 mL
Granulated sugar	2 tbsp.	30 mL
Salt	1/4 tsp.	1 mL
Large eggs, fork-beaten	4	4
Milk	2 cups	500 mL
Melted butter	3 tbsp.	50 mL
Grated orange zest (see Tip, page 122)	1/2 tsp.	2 mL
Cooking oil	1 tbsp.	15 mL

ORANGE BUTTER SAUCE

Butter	1/2 cup	125 mL
Granulated sugar	1/2 cup	125 mL
Orange juice	1/2 cup	125 mL
Grated orange zest (see Tip, page 122)	1 tbsp.	15 mL
Orange juice	2 tbsp.	30 mL
Cornstarch	2 tsp.	10 mL
Orange liqueur	2 tbsp.	30 mL

Crepes: Combine first 3 ingredients in large bowl. Make a well in centre.

Beat next 4 ingredients in medium bowl. Add to well. Whisk until smooth. Let stand for 1 hour. Stir.

Heat 1/4 tsp. (1 mL) cooking oil in small (8 inch, 20 cm) non-stick frying pan on medium. Pour about 2 tbsp. (30 mL) batter into pan. Immediately swirl batter to coat bottom, lifting and tilting pan to ensure entire bottom is covered. Cook until top is set and brown spots appear on bottom. Turn crepe over. Cook until brown spots appear on bottom. Transfer to plate. Repeat with remaining batter, heating more cooking oil if necessary to prevent sticking. Makes about 25 crepes (see Note).

Orange Butter Sauce: Melt butter in large frying pan on medium. Add next 3 ingredients. Heat and stir for about 2 minutes until sugar is dissolved and mixture starts to bubble.

Stir second amount of orange juice into cornstarch in small cup. Add to pan. Heat and stir until boiling and thickened. Remove from heat.

Add liqueur. Stir. Makes about 1 1/3 cups (325 mL) sauce. Fold each crepe in half, then in half again. Arrange crepes, slightly overlapping, on serving platter. Pour sauce over crepes. Serve immediately. Serves 10.

1 serving: 290 Calories; 16.4 g Total Fat (5.1 g Mono, 1.2 g Poly, 8.9 g Sat); 111 mg Cholesterol; 29 g Carbohydrate; trace Fibre; 6 g Protein; 198 mg Sodium

Pictured on pages 11 and at left.

Note: Crepes can be made ahead and kept at room temperature for a few hours until ready to serve. To reheat, stack crepes on a baking sheet or oven-proof platter and cover with foil. Place in 200°F (95°C) oven for about 1 hour until ready to serve. Serve topping in separate bowl.

Maple Rum Pears, below

Maple Rum Pears

Two types of cranberries provide contrasting but flavourful accents to roasted pears topped with a rich mascarpone rum sauce.

Maple (or maple-flavoured) syrup	1/3 cup	75 mL
Apple juice	1/4 cup	60 mL
Dark (navy) rum	1/4 cup	60 mL
Butter (or hard margarine), melted	2 tbsp.	30 mL
Lemon juice	1 tbsp.	15 mL
Ground cinnamon	1/2 tsp.	2 mL
Peeled pears, quartered	8	8
Dried cranberries	1 cup	250 mL
Fresh (or frozen, thawed) cranberries	1 cup	250 mL
Mascarpone cheese	10 oz.	285 g

Combine first 6 ingredients in large bowl.

Add next 3 ingredients. Toss until coated. Transfer to greased 9 x 13 inch (22 x 33 cm) baking dish. Spread evenly. Cover with foil. Bake in 375°F (190°C) oven for about 30 minutes until pears are tender. Transfer 1/3 cup (75 mL) cooking liquid to small bowl.

Add cheese to cooking liquid. Stir well. Serve with pear mixture. Serves 8.

1 serving: 385 Calories; 20.3 g Total Fat (0.7 g Mono, 0.1 g Poly, 10.7 g Sat); 52 mg Cholesterol; 49 g Carbohydrate; 5 g Fibre; 4 g Protein; 41 mg Sodium

Pictured on page 35 and above.

Variation: Instead of mascarpone cheese, serve with whipped topping or vanilla ice cream.

Rum Raisin Apple Enchiladas, right

Rum Raisin Apple Enchiladas

Filled with rum-drizzled apples, cinnamon and walnuts, and topped with a rich, buttery caramel sauce, these tortillas not only taste lovely but will smell heavenly as well. Serve with a scoop of vanilla ice cream or frozen yogurt.

Can of apple pie filling	19 oz.	540 mL
Sultana raisins	1/3 cup	75 mL
Chopped walnuts	2 tbsp.	30 mL
Dark (navy) rum (or 3/4 tsp., 4 mL, rum extract)	1 tbsp.	15 mL
Ground cinnamon	1 tsp.	5 mL
Flour tortillas (7 1/2 inch, 19 cm, diameter)	6	6

BUTTER RUM SAUCE

Brown sugar, packed	2/3 cup	150 mL
Butter (or hard margarine)	1/3 cup	75 mL
Granulated sugar	1/3 cup	75 mL
Whipping cream	1/4 cup	60 mL
Dark (navy) rum	2 tbsp.	30 mL
Water	2 tbsp.	30 mL
Vanilla extract	1 tsp.	5 mL

Combine first 5 ingredients in medium bowl.

Spoon apple mixture along centre of tortillas. Fold bottom ends of tortillas over filling. Fold in sides. Fold over from bottom to enclose filling. Place, seam-side down, in greased 9 x 13 inch (22 x 33 cm) baking dish.

Butter Rum Sauce: Combine first 6 ingredients in small saucepan. Bring to a boil on medium. Boil gently, uncovered, for 3 to 5 minutes, stirring constantly, until golden and slightly thickened.

Add vanilla. Stir. Makes about 1 1/2 cups (375 mL) sauce. Pour over tortillas. Let stand for 15 minutes. Bake in 350°F (175°C) oven for about 30 minutes until sauce is hot and bubbling. Serves 6.

1 serving: 555 Calories; 19.1 g Total Fat (5.8 g Mono, 2.5 g Poly, 9.7 g Sat); 39 mg Cholesterol; 90 g Carbohydrate; 3 g Fibre; 5 g Protein; 441 mg Sodium

Pictured at left.

Lemon Rhubarb Sour Cream Pie

A uniquely creamy and refreshing chilled dessert.

Sliced fresh (or frozen) rhubarb	2 cups	500 mL
Granulated sugar	3/4 cup	175 mL
Lemon juice	2 tbsp.	30 mL
Orange liqueur	2 tbsp.	30 mL
Large egg	1	1
Milk	1 cup	250 mL
All-purpose flour	2 tbsp.	30 mL
Grated lemon zest (see Tip, page 122)	2 tsp.	10 mL
Butter (or hard margarine)	2 tbsp.	30 mL
Envelope of unflavoured gelatin (about 1 tbsp., 15 mL)	1/4 oz.	7 g
Cold water	1/4 cup	60 mL
Sour cream	1/2 cup	125 mL
Graham cracker crust (see Note 1)	1	1
Frozen whipped topping, thawed	1 1/2 cups	375 mL
Strips of lemon peel, for garnish		

Combine first 4 ingredients in small saucepan on medium. Bring to a boil. Reduce heat to low. Cook, covered, for about 15 minutes, stirring occasionally, until rhubarb is very soft.

Whisk next 4 ingredients in small bowl. Slowly add to rhubarb mixture, stirring constantly. Increase heat to medium. Cook and stir for about 5 minutes, until boiling and thickened. Remove from heat.

Add butter. Stir until melted.

Sprinkle gelatin over cold water in separate small saucepan. Let stand for 1 minute. Heat and stir on low until gelatin is dissolved. Add to rhubarb mixture. Stir. Let stand for about 45 minutes until cooled completely.

Add sour cream. Mix well. Spread evenly in graham crust. Chill for about 4 hours until set (see Note 2).

Spoon whipped topping over top. Garnish with lemon peel. Cuts into 6 wedges.

1 wedge: 483 Calories; 22.5 g Total Fat (7.1 g Mono, 3.2 g Poly, 11.1 g Sat); 52 mg Cholesterol; 65 g Carbohydrate; 1 g Fibre; 6 g Protein; 313 mg Sodium

Pictured on page 41 and below.

Note 1: If you make your own crust, use a 9 inch (22 cm) deep dish pie plate.

Note 2: In a bit of a hurry? Freeze pie for about 1 hour until set instead of chilling.

Lemon Rhubarb Sour Cream Pie, above

Rich Cognac Custard

Rich, creamy custard with decadent cognac caramel sauce makes a perfect ending to any meal.

COGNAC CUSTARD

Egg yolks (large)	3	3
Large egg	1	1
Granulated sugar	1/3 cup	75 mL
Cognac (or brandy)	1/4 cup	60 mL
Vanilla extract	1 tsp.	5 mL
Whipping cream	1 1/2 cups	375 mL
Homogenized milk	1/2 cup	125 mL

COGNAC CARAMEL SAUCE

Caramel ice cream topping	1/4 cup	60 mL
Cognac	1 tsp.	5 mL

Cognac Custard: Grease six 1/2 cup (125 mL) ovenproof ramekins. Place in ungreased 9 x 13 inch (22 x 33 cm) baking dish. Set aside. Beat first 5 ingredients in medium bowl.

Combine whipping cream and milk in small saucepan. Heat on medium, stirring occasionally, until hot, but not boiling. Add 1/4 cup (60 mL) hot cream mixture to egg mixture. Stir. Slowly add egg mixture to remaining hot cream mixture, stirring constantly with whisk until well combined. Pour into prepared ramekins. Pour boiling water into baking dish until halfway up sides of ramekins. Bake in 300°F (150°C) oven for about 35 minutes until custard is set along edges but centre still wobbles. Carefully remove ramekins from water. Place on wire rack to cool. Chill, uncovered, for about 4 hours until cold.

Cognac Caramel Sauce: Combine ice cream topping and cognac in small cup. Makes about 1/4 cup (60 mL) sauce. Drizzle over chilled Cognac Custards. Serves 6.

1 serving: 348 Calories; 24.8 g Total Fat (7.7 g Mono, 1.3 g Poly, 14.4 g Sat); 205 mg Cholesterol; 22 g Carbohydrate; 0 g Fibre; 5 g Protein; 77 mg Sodium

Orange Rhubarb Mousse Cups

These individual tangy mousse cups are a refreshing end to any meal.

Chopped fresh (or frozen, thawed) rhubarb	2 cups	500 mL
Water	1/2 cup	125 mL
Frozen concentrated orange juice, thawed	1/4 cup	60 mL
Granulated sugar	2 tbsp.	30 mL
Ground cinnamon	1/8 tsp.	0.5 mL
Box of orange jelly powder (gelatin)	3 oz.	85 g
Grated orange zest	1/2 tsp.	2 mL
Salt, just a pinch		
Egg whites (large), see Safety Tip 1	2	2
Granulated sugar	2 tbsp.	30 mL
Orange segments, for garnish		

Combine first 5 ingredients in small saucepan. Bring to a boil. Reduce heat to medium. Boil gently, uncovered, for about 8 minutes, stirring occasionally, until thickened. Remove from heat.

Add jelly powder. Stir. Cool slightly. Carefully process with hand blender or in blender until smooth (see Safety Tip 2). Transfer to large bowl. Add orange zest and salt. Stir. Chill for 15 minutes. Beat egg whites in medium bowl until soft peaks form. Add second amount of sugar, 1 tbsp. (15 mL) at a time, beating constantly until stiff peaks form and sugar is dissolved. Fold half of egg white mixture into rhubarb mixture until just combined. Fold in remaining egg white mixture until no white streaks remain. Spoon into six 6 oz. (170 mL) ramekins. Spread evenly. Chill, covered, for about 1 hour until set. Dip ramekins into warm water for 20 to 30 seconds to loosen mousse. Invert onto serving plates, shaking gently to release. Garnish with orange segments. Serves 6.

1 serving: 116 Calories; 0.1 g Total Fat (trace Mono, 0.1 g Poly, trace Sat); 0 mg Cholesterol; 27 g Carbohydrate; 1 g Fibre; 3 g Protein; 72 mg Sodium

Pictured on page 55 and at left.

Safety Tip 1: This recipe uses raw eggs. Make sure to use fresh, uncracked, clean Grade A eggs. Pregnant women, young children or the elderly are advised not to eat anything containing raw egg.

Safety Tip 2: Follow blender manufacturer's instructions for hot liquids. If in doubt, we recommend using a hand blender.

Orange Rhubarb Mousse Cups, right

Chocolate Orange Chiffon Cake

This light-as-air cake served with orange liqueur whipped cream will turn any evening into a special occasion. Use eggs brought to room temperature for best results.

Cake flour	1 3/4 cups	425 mL
Granulated sugar	1 3/4 cups	425 mL
Cocoa, sifted if lumpy	1/3 cup	75 mL
Baking powder	1 tbsp.	15 mL
Salt	1 tsp.	5 mL
Baking soda	1/4 tsp.	1 mL
Egg whites (large)	7	7
Cream of tartar	1/2 tsp.	2 mL
Egg yolks (large), fork-beaten	7	7
Cooking oil	1/2 cup	125 mL
Orange juice	1/2 cup	125 mL
Grated orange zest	1 tsp.	5 mL
Vanilla extract	1 tsp.	5 mL
ORANGE WHIPPED CREAM		
Whipping cream	1 1/2 cups	375 mL
Icing (confectioner's) sugar	2 tbsp.	30 mL
Orange liqueur	2 tbsp.	30 mL

Measure first 6 ingredients into sieve over large bowl. Sift into bowl. Make a well in centre. Set aside.

Beat egg whites and cream of tartar in separate large bowl until stiff peaks form.

Add next 5 ingredients to well in flour mixture. Beat until smooth. Fold about 1/4 of egg white mixture into flour mixture. Add remaining egg white mixture in 2 additions, folding gently after each addition until no white streaks remain. Spread in ungreased 10 inch (25 cm) angel food tube pan. Bake in 325°F (160°C) oven for about 1 hour until wooden pick inserted in centre of cake comes out clean. Invert cake in pan onto glass bottle for 2 to 3 hours until cooled completely (see Note). Turn upright. Run knife around inside edge of pan to loosen cake. Remove bottom of pan with cake. Run knife around bottom, around tube and bottom of pan to loosen. Remove cake to large serving plate.

Orange Whipped Cream: Beat all 3 ingredients in small bowl until soft peaks form. Makes about 3 cups (750 mL) whipped cream. Serve with cake. Cuts into 16 wedges.

1 wedge with 3 tbsp. (50 mL) whipped cream: 310 Calories; 17.2 g Total Fat (7.3 g Mono, 2.7 g Poly, 6.2 g Sat); 112 mg Cholesterol; 35 g Carbohydrate; 1 g Fibre; 5 g Protein; 250 mg Sodium

Pictured on page 61 and below.

Peach Melba Gels, below

Peach Melba Gels

Peaches and raspberries are showcased in this delightful treat for the eyes and the tastebuds.

Chopped, drained canned peach slices	2 cups	500 mL
Fresh raspberries	1 1/2 cups	375 mL
White grape juice	1 1/2 cups	375 mL
Dry sherry	1/2 cup	125 mL
Granulated sugar	1/4 cup	60 mL
Envelope of unflavoured gelatin (about 1 tbsp., 15 mL)	1/4 oz.	7 g

Spoon peaches into 6 fruit cups or parfait glasses. Spoon raspberries over top. Chill.

Combine next 3 ingredients in small saucepan. Sprinkle gelatin over top. Let stand for 1 minute. Heat and stir on medium until gelatin is dissolved. Remove from heat. Cool to room temperature. Slowly pour over fruit in cups, allowing juice mixture to fill spaces. Chill for about 3 hours until set. Serves 6.

1 serving: 164 Calories; 0.4 g Total Fat (trace Mono, 0.1 g Poly, 0.1 g Sat); 0 mg Cholesterol; 38 g Carbohydrate; 4 g Fibre; 1 g Protein; 15 mg Sodium

Pictured above.

Chocolate Orange Chiffon Cake, above

DIY Pizza, page 49

Roasted Red Pepper Dip,
page 77

Tomato And Basil Salad,
page 123

Pink Pineapple Refresher,
page 91

Measurement Tables

Throughout this book measurements are given in Conventional and Metric measure. To compensate for differences between the two measurements due to rounding, a full metric measure is not always used. The cup used is the standard 8 fluid ounce. Temperature is given in degrees Fahrenheit and Celsius. Baking pan measurements are in inches and centimetres as well as quarts and litres. An exact metric conversion is given on this page as well as the working equivalent (Standard Measure).

OVEN TEMPERATURES

Fahrenheit (°F)	Celsius (°C)
175°	80°
200°	95°
225°	110°
250°	120°
275°	140°
300°	150°
325°	160°
350°	175°
375°	190°
400°	205°
425°	220°
450°	230°
475°	240°
500°	260°

DRY MEASUREMENTS

Conventional Measure Ounces (oz.)	Metric Exact Conversion Grams (g)	Metric Standard Measure Grams (g)
1 oz.	28.3 g	28 g
2 oz.	56.7 g	57 g
3 oz.	85.0 g	85 g
4 oz.	113.4 g	125 g
5 oz.	141.7 g	140 g
6 oz.	170.1 g	170 g
7 oz.	198.4 g	200 g
8 oz.	226.8 g	250 g
16 oz.	453.6 g	500 g
32 oz.	907.2 g	1000 g (1 kg)

PANS

Conventional Inches	Metric Centimetres
8 x 8 inch	20 x 20 cm
9 x 9 inch	22 x 22 cm
9 x 13 inch	22 x 33 cm
10 x 15 inch	25 x 38 cm
11 x 17 inch	28 x 43 cm
8 x 2 inch round	20 x 5 cm
9 x 2 inch round	22 x 5 cm
10 x 4 1/2 inch tube	25 x 11 cm
8 x 4 x 3 inch loaf	20 x 10 x 7.5 cm
9 x 5 x 3 inch loaf	22 x 12.5 x 7.5 cm

SPOONS AND CUPS

SPOONS

Conventional Measure	Metric Exact Conversion Millilitre (mL)	Metric Standard Measure Millilitre (mL)
1/8 teaspoon (tsp.)	0.6 mL	0.5 mL
1/4 teaspoon (tsp.)	1.2 mL	1 mL
1/2 teaspoon (tsp.)	2.4 mL	2 mL
1 teaspoon (tsp.)	4.7 mL	5 mL
2 teaspoons (tsp.)	9.4 mL	10 mL
1 tablespoon (tbsp.)	14.2 mL	15 mL

CUPS

	Metric Exact Conversion Millilitre (mL)	Metric Standard Measure Millilitre (mL)
1/4 cup (4 tbsp.)	56.8 mL	60 mL
1/3 cup (5 1/3 tbsp.)	75.6 mL	75 mL
1/2 cup (8 tbsp.)	113.7 mL	125 mL
2/3 cup (10 2/3 tbsp.)	151.2 mL	150 mL
3/4 cup (12 tbsp.)	170.5 mL	175 mL
1 cup (16 tbsp.)	227.3 mL	250 mL
4 1/2 cups	1022.9 mL	1000 mL (1 L)

CASSEROLES

CANADA & BRITIAN

Standard Size Casserole	Exact Metric Measure
1 qt. (5 cups)	1.13 L
1 1/2 qts. (7 1/2 cups)	1.69 L
2 qts. (10 cups)	2.25 L
2 1/2 qts. (12 1/2 cups)	2.81 L
3 qts. (15 cups)	3.38 L
4 qts. (20 cups)	4.5 L
5 qts. (25 cups)	5.63 L

UNITED STATES

Standard Size Casserole	Exact Metric Measure
1 qt. (4 cups)	900 mL
1 1/2 qts. (6 cups)	1.35 L
2 qts. (8 cups)	1.8 L
2 1/2 qts. (10 cups)	2.25 L
3 qts. (12 cups)	2.7 L
4 qts. (16 cups)	3.6 L
5 qts. (20 cups)	4.5 L

Recipe Index

Tiger Butter Bark, page 146